Creating the Colonial Administration
Economic Transition Following Abolition
Colonial Identity and State Power
Establishing Domination

Section II:
The Function and Creation of Classes within the Protectorate 1897-1926

The Decline of the Landowning Class
Politicalization of Racial Terms
The Function of the Power Bloc
through Colonial Ideology
Resistance, Identity, and Consciousness

Section III:
The Formative Development and Function of Political Parties 1926-1945
Establishment of the Political Structure
Communal Associations,
The Birth of Civil Society
Economic Development of the Shirazi
And their Resistance
Colonial State Economic
Institutions and Policies

Section IV:
Zanzibar During the Time of Politics and the Onset of Revolution 1945-1964

Avenues for Agency in
Response to Food Rationing
The Emergence and Political
Development of Nationalism
Party Development, Breakups
and Alliances
The Elections of 1961
The July 1963 Election and Its Aftermath
Conclusion:
Post-Independent Zanzibar

And the Victorious Triumph of John Okello

Bibliography
List of Tables
Table 1: Mainland Labor Population: 1923-1931
Table 2: Average Annual Customs Revenue
Table 3: Population of the Arab Community 1924-1948
Table 4: 1931 Government Survey of Landownership
Table 5: 1948 Baston Survey of Land Ownership
Tables 6 & 7: African Population Composition 1924-1948
Table 8: Population of Ethnic Communities in 1948
Table 9: 1957 Election Results for the Legislative Council
Table 10: Distribution of Seats in the Legislative Council January and June 1961
Table 11: Distribution of Seats in the Legislative Council July 1963

INTRODUCTION

The legacy of British imperialism in Zanzibar may be characterized by the term "divide and rule." This practice functioned by dividing subjects into racial groups and ruling them through managed conflicts among these "races." This is a legacy one finds in Zanzibar, as well as other British colonies. However, "divide and rule" did not fully exhaust British colonial practices. Indeed, they may have often been employed to obscure underlying historical circumstances. For most of the 16th and 17th centuries, the islands of Zanzibar and Pemba, along with a large swath of coastal East Africa, oscillated between long periods of Portuguese and Omani rule. Wars between these two dominating powers resulted in a constant change of allegiances by members of the ruling elite in Zanzibar. Final victory was firmly placed in the hands of the Omanis by the December of 1698 and their absolute rule continued unabated until the mid-nineteenth century. During the reign of Sayyid Sa'id bin Sultan al-Busaid in the mid-nineteenth century, the capital of the Omani sultanate was moved from Masqat to Zanzibar Town in order to better facilitate and manage the coastal slave trade; following his death in 1856, a power struggle occurred between his two sons as each sought to their consolidate power.[1] Reconciliation was requested and so the Governor-General of India, Lord Charles Canning, was called upon to adjudicate the matter; he ruled that the sons, Thuwaini and Majid, should separately rule the domains of Masqat and Zanzibar respectively.[2]

Coming upon the heels of internal power struggles across the islands, Zanzibar and its Sultan were recognized as sovereign and independent by Great Britain, France and Germany in 1862. With the succession of Sultan Barghash to the throne in 1870, he sought to capitulate on the Hamerton Treaty signed by Sultan Sayyid Sa'id in 1845, which prohibited the trading of slaves of Christian subjects in the Sultan's dominions, and the further promise of limiting slave trading within the Sultan's ports. Following "threats from the British Consul-General, Sir John Kirk...Barghash signed the treaty on 5 June 1873," immediately ruling that the slave trade, though not slavery, was illegal.[3] As such, this did not change the actual relationship between landlords and slaves on the islands as slaves continued to be the primary source of labor during harvest seasons and retained no rights.

Since the British had effectively extended their control over the territory for the better part of half a century, there was little the Sultan could do to restrain their grabs for power. The Delimitation Treaty, signed between Britain and Germany in late October 1886, sealed the extent of the Sultan's powers and the future status he would come to exercise.[4] Though continuing to recognize the Sultan as ruler and sovereign of Zanzibar and Pemba, the British sought to increase their power over the islands' domains in concert with Germany's expansion into the hinterland of mainland Africa. By 1890, with the signing of the treaty of Heligoland, Germany formally recognized Britain's protection over Zanzibar, while the former gained the territory of Heligoland.[5] From 1890 until December 1963, the British colonial administration ruled Zanzibar indirectly as a Protectorate, though employing various means of administrative, legislative and coercive tactics in order to ensure their rule remained unchallenged.

During this period, a primitive form of capitalism was introduced and a categorical division of society was instituted based upon perceived racial historiography. The British method of divide and indirect rule resulted in an alliance between their class of administrators and the decaying class of Arab landowners whose economic might collapsed following the Anglo-Zanzibar War of 27 August 1896 (and Sultan Khalid bin Barghash's loss) and the subsequent abolition of slavery in 1897. In order to effectively maintain indirect control and prevent social unrest, the British instituted practices and polices to artificially preserve the socio-political power of the landowners, even though the cost of securing their economic well being directly threatened the institutions of the colonial state.[6] Even as the British administration, through their alliance with Arab landowners, further entrenched racially driven policies, the advancement of capitalist mechanisms of agricultural production and ownership dramatically increased the ability of former slaves to acquire small landholdings. This divided the former class of slaves into an urban semi-proletariat working class and a smallholding class whose racial composition was not clean-cut, but rather was stratified across various categories.

Since the racial policies of the British administration did little to foster economic empowerment of the landowning class, even as their lands were being increasingly subdivided and sold off, landowners found themselves in a precarious position. Following the conclusion of World War II, and the racial-hierarchical practices of rationing throughout the Protectorate during the war years, landowners realized that it could only maintain its alliance in the power bloc by distancing themselves from the British and seek a new partnership. The emergence of the powerful smallholding class found common economic interests with Arab landowners that superseded the racially divided policies of the British. This alliance constituted a common discourse between the dominant economic producers within the Protectorate. However, their alliance proved that mere economic domination did not provide the necessary conditions for establishing hegemonic control once Zanzibar obtained independence. The success of the new power bloc alliance in elections on the eve of independence quickly faced resistance from the political opposition.[7]

On January 12, 1964, less than a month after achieving political independence as a fully constituted state, and after centuries of foreign rule, Zanzibar experienced a bloody revolution organized by a small, radical group of African mainlanders that spontaneously spread across the islands. By sunset, the post-independence government collapsed, the Sultan fled to mainland Africa, and one party rule was instituted. On April 26, 1964, the Revolutionary government agreed to an alliance with the neighboring nation of Tanganyika and formed the state of the United Republic of Tanzania. Though Zanzibar retained a large degree of autonomy in the new state, the hard won struggle for independence, begun nearly two decades earlier in nationalist activism against the colonialists, suddenly ceased to represent Zanzibar. The Revolution culminated into a chaotic period of racial strife, pitting the newly dominant African majority government against the small landowning Arab elite, the consequences of which were a direct result of the practices that had become institutionalized within the Protectorate during the colonial period.

To better understand and articulate the complex relationships that existed prior to the revolution of January 1964, it is necessary to postulate and examine the socially constructed identities of the peoples who inhabited the islands of the Protectorate as they were shaped through economic positions. Rather than rearticulate the oversimplified narrative of the Revolution as an event born out of racial turmoil, I propose to engage in a reexamination of the factors and conditions that contributed to the Revolution through colonial mandates created for the benefit of a small elite. The true circumstances underlying 73 years of British rule stem from class relations; these socially created privileges or exclusions resulted in the development of ethno-political tensions that fostered spontaneous and calamitous action. This precipitated into a "crisis of authority"[8] which, once the British administration withdrew its protective security domination, the authority of the ruling alliance quickly collapsed. Practices of economic exclusion and systematic exploitation of the majority of the population, drawn along racial lines, became internalized manifestations.

Method of Analysis and Statement of Inquiry

Antonio Gramsci's theory of hegemony rests within the historical conditions of medieval and post-Enlightenment Europe and the creation of institutions that allowed for the incubation of capitalism. These institutions were necessary for the formation of political education and economic privilege. The relationships of power, between a ruling class and their subaltern, do not exist within a vacuum, but rather are concretely manifested under unique circumstances, even if those individuals whose interests are invested within these relations are unaware of their exact nature.

The formation of a ruling class, and ultimately a political party, whose power extends across an entire society is not particularly simple. However, by applying the Gramscian terms of hegemony[9] versus domination, class, and the political party, to a particular structure, it becomes easier to comprehend the progression from a pre-capitalist relationship of power to one of "colonial capitalism", which culminated in a bloody revolutionary overthrow of the power bloc.

Simply, the term colonial capitalism refers to the state of economic affairs and production within the colonial territory that is based in part upon a reliance on mercantilism and the exploitation of peasant labor. In the instance of Zanzibar, the British Protectorate, by abolishing the institution of slavery, effectively destroyed the landowning elite's property rights over slaves. They lost their material basis for profit making through the exploitation of slave labor. This served a dual purpose as follows: the mass of peasants created by the abolishment of slavery were not only an expendable and exploitable labor pool, they were also consumers. By paying former slaves a piece wage for their physical labor the landowners were able to continue clove production and sustain exports. Through taxation of exported cash crops, the State was able to pay for the import of commodities such as cloth, oils, fuels, and foodstuffs, which the laborers quickly regarded as basic goods. These goods were purchased with their piece wages acquired through agricultural work. The abolition of slavery effectively created and sustained a class who developed into smallholder farmers through the accumulation of capital; these included: agricultural wage workers (*shamba*) [10] with squatter's rights that were largely a mirror of plantation slave practices. The *shamba* workers were allowed to remain on plots of land between clove and coconut trees, which they would be responsible for maintaining, and allowed to grow food and cash crops for their families or market; in exchange for land use privileges, *shamba workers* agreed to work during the harvest season and would generally earn wages. In addition to *shamba* workers, a class of urban semi-proletarian workers developed with limited protected land rights under *aqwaaf* that had been setup by Sultans for former slaves and servants.[11]

Following the abolition of slavery:

"measures were taken to ensure that the transition to free labour would not upset property relations. Owners received monetary compensation for the property they lost in persons, while their control of clove plantations was not disturbed. Many ex-slaves, unable to find land outside the plantation sector, were bonded with former masters as squatters on old estates. They were joined by peasants and migrants to form the labour force in the export sector of the colonial economy."[12]

The advent of a hierarchy of social classes who were able to acquire capital, under the tutelage of the Sultan and the protection of the Protectorate, but who "did not become a landless proletariat as in classical capitalism" created conditions that can be termed, colonial capitalism.[13]

By examining the colonial relationship that came into being after 1890 in the British protectorate of Zanzibar, I will follow the historical formation of class as it developed through mandated policies of the Protectorate. In turn, the construction of class identity developed into one of political struggle for power of the State following the period after World War II as the advent of political parties articulated an ideology of Zanzibari nationalism. To understand how class and political struggle ultimately culminated in a bloody Revolution after merely one month of independence, I will concretely apply Gramsci's terms of domination and its various manifestations as it is understood in opposition to hegemony.[14] However, I shall not be employing directly Gramsci's materialist theory; rather, I will use Gramsci in an idealist non-Marxist manner in order to emphasize and highlight identity formation more than the material interests of various classes. I will undertake this examination in order to answer the following questions:

How it is possible that the colonial partnership of a power bloc alliance between the landowning class and dominant British class collapsed? Out of its remains, a new power bloc was formed among landowners, petite-bourgeoisie merchants, and smallholders. Why was this power bloc, which represented the interests of the dominant economic classes, overthrown within a month of its independent mandate? What were the historical and socio-economic conditions that allowed for this postcolonial power bloc to emerge? Equally as important and intriguing is how it was possible for one individual, John Okello, to mobilize and successfully organize a grassroots revolution within the rural countryside of the islands.

Terms of Power

Central to the Gramscian analysis are four terms: ruling class, dominant class, power bloc, and historic bloc. Ruling class is the class that supplies political rulers, but which may or may not have the coercive or political means necessary to establish dominance within the Protectorate. Under the royal family, Al Bu Sa'id, the ruling clan during the Sultanate, political and economic institutions were not clearly differentiated with Arab landowners and slave owners constituting part of a ruling class. Under the Protectorate, British colonial administrators were the ruling class (which assigned the Sultan as its deputy, thus part of the ruling class). The dominant class is that class which dominates the material life of the society. During the period of the Sultanate, Arab landowners formed the dominant class. Under the Protectorate, Indian merchants were increasingly dominant economically, fully replacing Arab landowners as the dominant class by the early 1900s. A dominant class provides the material basis for rule to the ruling class when they are in alliance with one another. This alliance is called the power bloc when this alliance is an official partnership. When the dominant class acquiesces and is not an official partner to the ruling class, the latter assumes the power of ruling without a power bloc. The dominant class supplies the ruling class with its absences and enforces not only the physical security role, but provides legitimacy to the government and the ruling class. Together, these two classes come to constitute the power bloc.

The power bloc itself does not constitute a historic bloc, nor does it have the ability to acquire hegemony within the institutions of government. Rather, the power bloc exists in so far as it is able to maintain political order and at the very least maintain the socio-economic interests of its allied classes. Conversely, the historic bloc is formed when two disparate classes find commonalities that outweigh any differences in material interests. Moreover, the historic bloc is only able to form under circumstances relating to the political, but which are formed in the economic. However, since the political and economic institutions were not separate, but constituted as one-in-the-same under the Sultanate, the introduction of capitalism following the abolition of slavery under the Protectorate saw the beginning of a differentiation of these two institutions. A power bloc became the only outcome under these circumstances and prevented the emergence of a historic bloc since capitalism never fully developed until after independence.[15]

The classes that came to constitute the postcolonial power bloc, in the case of Zanzibar, were the large landowning elites along with smallholder peasants who were brought into a position of power not only through their economic holdings, but also by garnering political support throughout the islands. The development of colonial capitalism provided the means possible through which the alliance between landowners and smallholders transcended socio-political differences of exclusion in order to constitute a new power bloc. Their related economic interests allowed for a dialogue to be established that articulated the demands of both classes and overcame socially conditioned divisions created by the colonial administration. In understanding the emergence and development of the new power bloc and their establishment of power within the postcolonial State, it is necessary to examine the function of power prior to independence, which was the domination of the State through the power bloc. As noted above, and will be further development in Section I, domination and hegemony are twin terms that require fundamentally different structures of power in which to operate and develop.

Revolutionary Developments

Contrary to the numerous analysis of the Revolution declaring that colonial Zanzibar was fraught with racial tensions that ultimately drove the country into chaos, I will show that, in fact, the racial categories employed by the British were merely superficial, fluid and effervescent terms that obscured the actual nature of class formations; these categories were further devised as a discursive part of the ruling mechanism of "divide and rule." It was these class formations and their identification and association with political parties during the "period of politics" in the 1950s that ultimately lead to an extreme division of inequality on the islands of Zanzibar and Pemba.

However, the tensions among Arab landowners, Shirazi smallholders, and African mainland laborers that existed on Zanzibar that were the source of conflict in the run-up to independence were largely absent on Pemba Island. The extreme violence following the Revolution of 1964 was heavily concentrated on Zanzibar, while Arab and Shirazi landowners on Pemba maintained relatively peaceful relationships due to a history of intermarriage and communal relationships. Due to this factor, the assertions that Zanzibar was fraught with racial tensions that led directly to the Revolution often exclude the relationships that existed on Pemba. The alliance between the Zanzibar and Pemba People's Party (ZPPP) and Zanzibar National Party (ZNP) during elections in the 1960s, is most notable for the fact that it was formed on common economic interests of the landowning and bourgeois classes not one premised on racial unity. The interests of classes and their economic well being superseded any communal or historical allegiances, at least on Pemba.

The outbreak of the Revolution occurred not through a charge of the African masses who felt dejected by their status, but rather through the organized actions of one man, John Okello. The ability of this one leader, whose "swiftness in connecting seemingly disparate facts, and in conceiving the means adequate to particular ends—thus discovering the interests involved, and arousing the passions of men and directing them towards a particular action," was made possible only through the process of a war of movement, and a "crisis of authority" within the ruling class.[16] It is a gross oversimplification to suggest that racial tensions culminated in a revolution. Though social conditions were certainly apparent and did contribute to the disenfranchisement of the majority, it fails to take into account the historical circumstances that came into existence after the declaration of the Protectorate and subsequent shift in the social structure of the islands through the abolition of slavery in 1897.[17]

In order to deconstruct the formation of political parties, and their function in necessitating the Revolution, I will approach the material cause through Gramscian terms as he defined and analyzed political parties, but within an idealist non-Marxist framework. Clearly laying out the historical development of economic classes among the populations of Zanzibar and Pemba in the period following the abolition of slavery, it will be possible to locate a moment of intersection in which the demands of the colonial administrative class, and their allied landowning class, ultimately became coupled and were able to formulate policy within the colonial state as a power bloc. However, this coincided with the subordination of the all other classes, even those (such as merchants) whose economic might superseded that of the dominant landowning class.

The interests of the smallholder and urban working classes diverged separately from that of the colonial state as each group had a constituted interest based on their relationship to landownership. This became legally manifest through the British practice and policy of Zanzibar being constituted solely as an Arab state, even if this fundamental application was not within the economic interests of the majority of classes.[18] This allows for an understanding of the political parties as they came to exist and how they emerged from within a particular class structure. These parties ultimately utilized (in a deliberately methodological manner) and exploited categories of race and tradition to classify and isolate the population. The under-privileged came to define itself in opposition not only to their marginalization based on economic dependency and exploitation, but against the entire social structure of power from which they had been systematically excluded and continued to demean their essential well-being.

The consequences of State sanctioned socio-economic privilege of the landowning class provide the most concrete method for understanding the formation of political parties in Zanzibar during the 1950s. Social tensions became increasingly unsustainable as parties sought to define themselves according to racial commonalities, as well as differences, due to the internalization of race through political education. The political parties as such were constructed from within particular classes: landowners, urban and rural workers, smallholders, and merchants. Unsurprisingly, the landowners were the first class to become conscious of the need for political legitimacy in the face of increasing pressure for an emerging bourgeois merchant class. [19]

Increasing economic rivalry between formerly ruling landowners during the Sultanate and the dominant merchants under the Protectorate resulted in the latter being denied access to political representation in the colonial state under the premise that their economic privileges would be maintained by the former class.[20] However, the class of landowners was not alone in administering the affairs of the State and their position depended almost entirely on their alliance with the British. The British exercised control of the

Protectorate in order to establish a stable order through the apparatus of a ruling class.

Identification, Definition, and Categorization

In order for the dominant but declining landowning class during the post-slave society of the Protectorate to define itself as a superior group through not only material conditions, but also by their political and social dominance, the class must find, create and construct a group or community of 'others' whose practices are termed archaic and whose members are able to be willingly subordinated through categories that designate them as such. [21] This willingness often transpires without the 'other' in fact knowing or becoming conscious of their existence as one of subordinate status since their complacency creates the conditions necessary to undermine their position in the political, social and economic realms. These conditions are possible through a complex system of economic exploitation along with disenfranchisement from the land and its direct relationship to production through the practice of political control by exclusion.[22] Moreover, these economic conditions are constrained, as well as challenged and influenced by the politico-ethical, which does not exist as independent of the colonial government, but depends upon it for access to agency. This form of agency can become manifested in manipulated circumstances that ultimately benefit the Protectorate and its ruling class.

It is only through brute force or resistance that the subaltern comes into consciousness of itself. Since the subaltern constitutes the great masses, they will ultimately prevail in a war of movement; however, they must take care to understand the particular economic conditions created by permanent situations of economic dependence.[23] These conditions were facilitated and reinforced by the power bloc whose interests lie in defining exact measures of economic production and profit in order to establish and maintain their domination through consent and economic dependency.

Before there can exist a relationship of power, there must exist prior a competition of economic forces which necessitates the need for one class to define itself as superior to that of another in order to justify the creation and employment of power relations. In order for this consciousness to exist, there must be "intellectuals" who are able to coalesce a class through definite boundaries so that they are able to distinguish what precisely sets them apart from other classes in order to either obtain or justify power.[24]

Until there exists in actuality a discourse that characterizes the circumstances in which the class finds itself, it is not able to take action or ascend to power. For until such terms can be ascribed for the circumstances in which the subordinate class finds itself, they remains unable to extricate itself from their position. Through the associated privileges that the Protectorate enacted during the early twentieth century, the dominant class eventually becomes cognizant that they are in a position of socio-political dominance over other classes.

This function of self-awareness takes form most concretely in the formation of class, and is directly tied to the relationship that exists between economic production and landownership. In becoming the dominant class, producers remain tethered to the relationship of economic production through access to landownership. It is through this exercise that they are able to ascribe positions and limits of power not only within their own class, but also among all other classes whose own consciousness of their position does not yet exist. Only through the exploitation of human labor as it relates to material production does the dominant class come to apply the terms of class and power to not only themselves, but the whole of society.

The class position of former-slaves exists only insofar as the landowning class has manifested itself within a system of power and extended their reach beyond that of simple force; the landowning class comes to define the entire structure of society through its own terms and by its own traditions disseminated through political education.[25] It is able to do so because once it has become aware of its class, in relation to that of other classes, it immediately undertakes the most direct route to socio-economic power, the apparatus of power in the Protectorate and its implicit dominance. In order for the landowning class to fully invest itself in the administration of the Protectorate in the period following the abolition of slavery, it was forced to form alliances with other classes. The lack of available and exploitable labor had immediately consequences for the well being of not only individual plantations, but also the socio-economic structure of the islands as a whole.

Landowners faced the severe consequences of owning thousands of trees filled with rotting cloves and coconuts because there were not enough willing laborers to harvest them. This great challenge was an unintended development of abolition that directly threatened the livelihood of landowners who found themselves calling to action their power bloc partners, the British administration. In order to best resolve this predicament as quickly as possible, besides employing coercive methods as discussed in Sections II and III, landlords resolved to allow former slaves to continue to live upon the plantation land, rent free, in exchange for harvesting and weeding the clove and coconut areas within which the squatters would plant their own food crops. This solution did not wholly benefit either landlords or the squatters over the long-term; by the 1920s it fell upon the British to resolve the questions of land tenure.

Since the relationship that exists between actors who control the means of production and those who facilitate its existence is one of power based upon the interests of the power bloc, the ability to theorize the necessity and employment of race as a category becomes possible. Race cannot be framed within a particular set of circumstances that is devoid or irrespective of the relationship between the racial composition of a class and their ability to exert and extract power from within the state sanctioned system. As noted by Sheriff:

"Because class formation cuts across racial boundaries, the ruling bourgeoisie uses ethnicity as an ideology to obscure class contradictions and misdirect class struggle. Race under capitalism becomes social as well as biological categories, and an important functional element in the socio-economic function," *Zanzibar Under Colonial Rule*, 145.

Though the two terms, class and race, diverge and intersect, they nonetheless are twin units of the same language that is being employed on the basis of power.[26]

Development of Colonial State Structures

Dealing with the institutional analysis of the formation of parties requires a review of the colonial system and its numerous manifestations of power. After the abolition of slavery, the colonial capitalist system became manifested and maintained across all segments of society; essentially reproduced itself according to one guiding principle, the ability to control or align labor forces in the cultivation of cash crops. In doing so, the power bloc shifted the *shamba* workers relationship to the land from one of labor exploitation for the harvesting of non-food crops with no land rights during slavery to that of labor exploitation for a piece-wage, along with limited land rights, including squatter's rights, after abolition. This is useful in understanding how it was possible for a class to form a political party based on factors that are inherently part of their social structure, but within categories that correspond to prescribed definitions of race; however, these terms ultimately dependent upon and are subject to broader social relationships.[27]

The emergence of colonial capitalism was fostered and instituted by the British after the collapse of exploitable labor following the abolition of slavery in 1897. The identification and category of slave remained, even after abolition, an unbridgeable status group or "caste" that could not be disregarded or overcome. Class was not an inherent category within Zanzibar prior to abolition, but rather was a new social condition created by the colonial power in order to enforce domination over the entire population, though with privileges for Arab landowners.[28] The structures that were sought out for destruction or expropriation during the Revolution were directly tied to the system of land exploitation, distribution, and economic enterprise. In seeking to reform the vestiges and apparatuses that had directly contributed to the exploitation of African peasants and laborers, the leaders of the Revolution fostered and created conditions of economic cooperation among all classes. Prior to their assent to power, they were able to successfully cultivate class alliances through a war of movement[29] by exploiting economic inequalities.

The socio-economic structures of the colonial state first functioned in order to ensure that the landowning class would retain their economically dominant positions as they had under the Sultanate; as capitalism developed more fully with the ascending merchant class, the dominant position of the landowners weakened to such a degree that by the 1920s the merchants had supplanted them as economically dominant. The landowners continued to retain their political privileges until the 1940s through their alliance with the British within the power bloc. The power bloc took advantage of the old social stratification. Instituted administrative practice and procedure within the Protectorate ensured that the underprivileged and less desirable class ("expendable") were subjugated according to the term of an "other". The identity of Africans as such became a racial category due to the fact that they were unable to express or locate themselves as being socially represented within the structures of power since historical circumstances continually marginalized them first as slaves, then as a subaltern class. Though their economic power increased through smallholdings, being categorized as African placed individuals at a socio-political disadvantage, which they were unable to resolve. They founded themselves on the basis of opposition due to their lack of voice, and in their quest for agency became defined according to the terms as constructed and employed by the Protectorate.

Not only being unaware, or at the very least dismissive of their subordinate socio-economic status, the class of former slaves and mainland Africans immigrants were hard pressed to select a predetermined racial identity as defined by the colonial administration during census taking procedures. Class becomes no more accessible than race when the conditions of labor exploitation do not allow workers such privileges of identification or definition of themselves. Remaining disenfranchised from the economic, as well as the political structures of power further reinforced the lack of solidarity across the African classes. The fluidity of racial terms employed by former slaves corresponded not to an actual category (since these had not existed in any concrete form or practice prior to the British Protectorate)[30] but to a perceived economic advantage by identifying oneself and community as belonging to a predetermined racial definition. Of course, this identification could and did change quickly over time according to the importance placed upon a hierarchical structure of economic privilege as it directly corresponded to "inequalities in the distribution of various symbolic and material resources."[31]

Structure of Analysis

In order to coherently organize this analysis according to the emergence of a stratified hierarchical class-based social structure, albeit one within the parameters of a colonial system, this paper will be divided categorically into four sections. The first will introduce the notion of hegemony as defined by Gramsci and how its practices can be used in identifying another form of power, domination, in the period immediately following establishment of the Protectorate in 1890. These definitions allow for an understanding of which form of power existed within the Protectorate and how the power blocs could be susceptible to insurrection against it.

After the abolition of slavery in 1897, discussed in Section II, the relationship between landowners and slaves that had existed under the Sultanate experienced a rupture that would continue to reshape the socio-economic institutions of the Protectorate until the mid-1920s. Race in itself does not intrinsically contribute to the economic well-being or status of a particular persons; rather race was employed and defined by the power bloc, whose access to economic privileges were greater, in order to constrain and confine into categories that which, while they may appear real, are best utilized for the advantage of the power bloc for itself. In short, racial markers simplify categories that are inherently complex and do not allow for an understanding or dissection of greater indicators that contributed to the end result of the colonial project in Zanzibar, the Revolution.

By clearly defining what domination, as well as hegemony, is and how it came into being, it will be possible to move to the second section, class. The emergence of class necessitates an order wherein one class exercises a dominant function over other subordinate classes through their control of the economic-political structures of the State. Non-ruling classes are, at least in the beginning, not aware of their status or exploitative position. Only by becoming familiar with and utilizing the discourse of the power bloc are they able to acquire consciousness of their position. This may occur in a flash or over many decades as the economic structure shifts and eventually erodes the power base of the ruling class until it becomes dominant in name only. This allows for a caveat of opposition to emerge and challenge the dictatorship of the power bloc.[32]

As political institutions came into existence according to class, as well by race, following the establishment of the Legislative Council in 1926, Section III will examine the implications of political representation throughout the 1930s and 1940s. The political party emerges from within a particular class and cannot but represent the interests of that class; though their appeal or reach may extend across socially constructed categories of difference, the party is nevertheless born out of and a product of a distinct class. The exercise and existence of the political party is solely for control of the institutions of the colonial administration in the interests of a particular class. [33] The fourth section will be a narrative analysis of Zanzibar during the post-war period, 1945-1964, which culminated into an increasingly divided society whose allegiance to the interests of the Protectorate were superseded by party identification.

Certain conditions existed in 1964 in order for a loosely coordinated act of violent opposition to occur. The reality of "human nature" is not one of "fixed and immutable" positions, but rather is "the totality of historically determined social relations" whose particular outcomes are contingent upon the ability to obtain or express power.[34] The need for segregation within the Protectorate among various particular social groups coincided with the emergence of class-based divisions of economic utility following abolition that functioned according to the practices of landownership. To the extent that this was fostered by the British colonial administration, in alliance with the landowning class, helps to place within a historical period of time the evolving and emerging conditions that created a system of domination through minority-rule class dictatorship. The denouement of Arab landowners resulted in a "crisis of authority" as "the ruling class…lost its consensus" and became "detached" from the existences of *shamba* squatters and economically powerful smallholders; the former no longer able to extract consent from the latter, who ultimately responding to the decaying conditions by a coordinated use of force.[35]

Section I: THE EMERGENCE AND ESTABLISHMENT OF DOMINATION IN THE BRITISH PROTECTORATE, 1890-1926

Pre-and Post-Abolition (1890-1910)

In order to layout and understand the immense upheaval which occurred in 1897 with the abolition of slavery, and the reinforcement of British primacy on the islands following the brief Anglo-Zanzibar war of 27 August 1896, it is necessary to briefly summarize the developments that led up to that moment and the shifts that is caused within the social structure of the Protectorate. Even before Sultan Sayyid Sa'id transferred his palace capital from Masqat to Zanzibar, he was subject to the imperial machinations of Great Britain who as early as 1822 sought to abolish the slave trade within the Sultan's domains. Though he signed the Moresby Treaty in 1822, along with other later trade agreements, notably the Hamerton Treaty in 1845, none were ever fully brought into force during his reign. While there are numerous reasons as to why the Sultan would acquiesce to such an agreement that ran entirely counter to the economic well being of his Sultanate (sultanah), not least of which being the might of the British Royal Navy, the Sultan did extract gains from his participation. The most significant outcome of the Moresby Treaty was the establishment of diplomatic relations with the United States in 1836, Britain in 1840, and with France shortly thereafter.[36]

During the period between the permanent establishment of the Sultan's palace in 1832 and Sayyid Sa'id's death in 1858, the social structure of Zanzibar experienced an influx of Arab settlers from Oman. They were driven in large part by the economic boom in the demand for cloves, which was built upon the backs of slavery. Not only did these Arabs settlers engage in clove and coconut cultivation through the creation of large landholdings, but were instrumental in sustaining the demand for slaves within the kingdom. While there is little information and research available on the land tenure that existed prior to the establishment of Arab-owned plantations, it is most likely that the majority of individuals enjoyed communal landholdings. This continued to be practiced on Pemba Island well into the 1950s, due to not only its distance from Zanzibar, but also the centralized structure that the Sultan established in Zanzibar Town proper continued to be practiced during the Protectorate.[37] The unique circumstances of Pemba allowed for communal landholdings to be commonplace and existed not only within African communities, but also existed between Arabs and Africans in the same communities. Also of important note is that although Sayyid Sa'id established full control over Zanzibar and most of the East Coast of Africa, it was not until later in his reign that Pemba was wrestled from control of Mombasa. As such, Pemba retained a relatively separate identity from the rest of Zanzibar and was not as actively engaged in the centralized power structures of the Sultan. While the slave trade certainly extended to Pemba, the main slave market was located directly in Zanzibar Town and its importance was more closely associated with the large number of urban Arabs.[38]

Once Arab settlers became engaged with the cultivation and production of cloves for export, they, by default, also actively participated in the exchange, buying and selling of slaves. It is not without coincidence that during the elections of 1963, rumors abounded that should the Arab bloc win the election they would immediately reinstitute slavery.[39] The historical association of slavery with the Arab landowners could never be fully erased in the minds of disenfranchised African majority. This fueled suspicion of collusion between Arab landowners and the British colonial administration for the indefinite denial of power to the Africans. The rights of slaves during this period were limited to their master's dictates.

Given the nature of the twice-annual monsoons that provide Zanzibar with its harvest seasons, there were only about four to six weeks of actual work to be done throughout the year, broken up into two periods of harvesting between which there was scant other work.[40] As such, slaves found themselves with long periods of relative autonomy during which they engaged in the cultivation of food crops for their own consumption, as well as fishing, craft making and handiwork. It was often the case that slaves and their masters agreed upon a four-to-five day work week with the other two-to-three days being set aside for the cultivation of food crops for personal and household consumption.

However, the winds of change began to blow and the British began to exert a strong force upon the successors to Sayyid Sa'id; it is not without coincidence that the British chose to breakup the Sultanate into two separate halves which both weakened the autonomy of each respective Sultan, while at the same time bringing the Sultanate of Zanzibar into closer allegiance to Britain. While the power of the Sultan became increasingly limited, it was not until the abolition of the slave trade within the Sultan's domains, signed in 1873, that the actual economic power and sustainability of the kingdom was curtailed. The dependence upon revenues from the slave trade, coupled with the devastating hurricane of 1872, meant that the Sultan could no longer resist the encroaching power of British authorities.[41] In compensation for the losses associated with the slave trade, the British created an annual salary to be paid to the Sultan, further distancing the position of the palace from socio-economic structure of the islands prior to the declaration of the Protectorate.

By the time of the establishment of the Protectorate in 1890, the burden of sustaining a significant labor force of slaves who were largely unproductive for the majority of the year had begun to sharply erode the profits of the Arab landowners. Feeding, clothing, and housing hundreds if not thousands of slaves was extremely inefficiently since, with the exception of a small minority of household slaves who worked year round, the agricultural slaves did not provide enough surplus value for the work they rendered. Moreover, due to the long periods of inactivity and the chronically poor health conditions coupled with extreme humidity and heat, many slaves did not make it past a year on the islands before succumbing to malaria, dysentery, or any other number of diseases. The large turnover of slaves required that landowners continually purchase new slaves each year to replace those they had lost, further digging into the meager profits.

Though the British campaign to abolish slavery was well established by the time they declared a Protectorate in Zanzibar, their difficulty in enforcing it on the islands became of paramount importance not so much based on morality (though that argument certainly is a valid, if not quite simplistic) but on the devastating effect slavery was having on the economy of the Protectorate. Since the British had assumed all profits and losses of the islands, the Sultan receiving an annual annuity, as well as all household expenses in compensation for his lack of authority, they could not abide by a social structure that did not provide for the greatest possible extraction of resources and profit for the minimal amount of labor required. The large numbers of slaves on the islands, who greatly outnumbered the Arab landowners, the Sultan's entourage and the British administrators, constituted a grave security threat that could implode at any moment; furthermore, they represented a collective group of individuals who did not directly contribute a surplus value to the economy.

Under terms signed by Al Bu Sa'id on the 1 August 1890, which prohibited the slave trade but not slavery itself, and established the Protectorate, the British administration was given veto power over the succession of future sultans.[42] This ensured that British could retain controls over the sultan and his cabinet by appointing only men who were on terms favorable to British interests. However, this ultimately culminated into a short-lived crisis of authority on 25 August 1896 when Sultan Hamad bin Thuwaini died unexpectedly under unclear circumstances and his 29 year-old nephew Khalid bin Barghash seized power. The British did not approve of Khalid as successor and informed him that he must immediately step down; Khalid proved unwilling to do so, despite repeated attempts and threats from the British the following day. At 9:00 a.m. on the 27th of August British gunships anchored in the harbor opened fire on the palace where Khalid had stationed himself and about 1,000 men. By 9:40 the entire palace complex was smoldering in ruins and Khalid had fled to the German embassy and sought asylum. That same day the British proclaimed a new sultan, Hamoud bin Mohammed.[43]

The immediate consequences of the war, often termed the shortest war in history, cannot be overstated. Not only did the new sultan capitulate and abolish slavery within less than a year on 6th of April 1897, but he owed his entire power and authority to the security of the British. Khalid had been able to muster a force of 1,000 men because much of the population was displeased with the agreement signed in 1890.[44] The British demonstrated to the peoples of Protectorate that they would not tolerate an act of defiance that ran counter to their interests and were prepared to use lethal force as necessary. The deaths of 500 Zanzibari men during the 40 minute bombardment had profound and devastating effects on the population who realized once and for all that they were no longer beholden to the authority of the sultan but solely to that of a foreign power.

The British could not rule through force alone however, nor did they have any intention of doing so when there were better methods for instituting indirect rule. In order to satisfy the demands of security and stabilize the shrinking profits of landowners, the British created a money economy in which former slaves would be paid a piece-wage for work rendered; in turn, this piece-wage would be used to purchase imported goods, as well as local foodstuffs, and provide a sustained demand for goods during the off-seasons.

However, the lack of available labor immediately following the abolition of slavery created problems that could not be solved simply by an influx of money. It is the case that "for capital to be productive, a constant supply of labor is required. If it is not available, the state will often resort to various means of making it available--including force if necessary, as was the case in Zanzibar."[45] Since labor could not simply be imported from the mainland, the colonial State devised financial incentives, with cooperation of landowners, in order to attract workers from the mainland whose wages were often far lower than those offered in the Protectorate.[46] This was comparatively easy since labor was only required for a few weeks out of the year and mainland workers would therefore be able to return home with their wages; however, this did not solve the problem of sustaining a domestic workforce who could be called upon quickly and who would retain their labor skills over time.

It was feared, before abolition, that domestic slaves, once freed, would simply forgo work on plantations and households in order to provide for their own domestic consumption; in the process this would devastate landowners as their workers had little incentive to obtain piece-wage labor when there was no demand for wages. In order to further minimize the demands for freedom following abolition in 1897, for abolition did not in itself immediately provide freedom, the British administration made it increasingly difficult for agricultural slaves to legally obtain their freedom. [47] This was mainly through enforcing rigorous bureaucratic hurdles and paperwork conducted overwhelmingly in English. Many individuals found it more advantageous to remain categorically a slave and retain some squatter rights to the land on which they lived.

Since economic incentives, though comparatively generous, ultimately failed to build-up or encourage a domestic labor force, coercive measures were undertaken and "a period of forced labour" became administrative practice in the Protectorate.[48] Not only were former slaves disinclined to undertake work (clove harvesting) that had previously been directly associated with slavery, but a large feeling of distrust had developed between former slaves and landowners further contributed to the lack of interest for piece-wages. At the same time, the British administration undertook projects of infrastructure building that further strained the already weak labor force. Within a decade of abolition, "every possibly forcible method was used. The people were driven from their homes...or made to go and pick cloves themselves until they produced a certain number of labourers."[49] In order for a system of capitalism to develop, both former slaves and their landowning masters had to be forced into becoming laborers and contribute to the social economy through wages, labor, and commoditization of imported goods.

The three decades immediately following the declaration of the Protectorate were precarious ones for landowners, as well as the emerging classes of former slaves who were eventually freed from the shackles of slavery. In order to maintain its official policy of indirect rule, the British needed to align themselves with the economically dominant class so that it could exercise a security function, but did not require a large colonial presence on the islands. However, the British, by the turn of the century, found that the established class of landowners were not secure in the economic position; in fact, following abolition, they were quickly losing their large plantations to increasingly dominant merchant class. This was due to a variety of factors such as indebtedness, Islamic inheritance proscriptions, and the inability to financially sustain a large labor force.

Landowner indebtedness to South-Asian merchants whose monopoly on the export of cloves to the two largest importers, India and Indonesia, allowed the merchants to exploit the need of landowners to raise capital at the beginning of the harvest season in order to pay for laborers. However, since the merchants controlled the export of cloves, they were able to manipulate prices to such a degree that landowners could not recoup enough profit in order to repay their loans. Each year, the loan from the previous year would be extended with additional interest incurred and another loan provided for the employment of laborers. This cyclical indebtedness became unsustainable by the end of the first decade of twentieth-century but a solution could not be determined until the 1920s. [50]

Further undermining the longevity of the large landowners were the tradition of Islamic inheritance rights by which the land is equally divided among all children with daughters receiving half as much as sons. While this ensured that no child or their offspring would be without land, shelter, and the ability to cultivate food crops, after a few generations of subdividing in this manner, plots became either too small or undesirable for cultivation. This proved problematic since Islamic law was and continues to be the basis of rule of law in Zanzibar and the British found it unwise to prohibit such practices. However, the British administration faced the dilemma of whether to continue to support the large landowning estates, who required far greater resources for their continuance, but whose allegiance to the Sultan and British was near absolute, or of whether to embrace the more efficient but far more numerous smallholders in order to prevent the collapse of the socio-economic structure.[51]

Ultimately the British decided that it, in order to stave off any messy social upheavals and chaos by allowing large landowners to become dispossessed from their lands, they would resolutely enact legislative policies, discussed further below, favoring the landowning class. They also realized that the economic future of the islands rested upon smallholders and that smallholding should be quietly encouraged, in order to create an economically vibrant class, even if they remained socially alienated from the colonial government.[52] While publically the British continued to express unconditional support of large landowners, even as it alienated merchants and moneylenders, the administration did enact financial schemes during the 1920s, with mixed results, that encouraged smallholders to plant new clove trees and further empower them to become small-scale capitalists. These contradictory measures undermined the ability of the British to fully maintain economic control of the export markets since they continually relied upon the acquiescence of the disenfranchised, but economically dominant merchant class.

Creating the Colonial Administration

In attempting to create and sustain the colonial Protectorate, necessary functions and positions of privilege were needed in order to successfully maintain not only the political and social affairs of the colonial state, but more importantly to exercise economic domination over the entire populace.[53] Social arrangements, as they are structured through economic functions, become expressed privileges with protection by the colonial state; these privileges are made possible with the alignment of a particular class within the administrative apparatus. Through the institutions of the Protectorate, the power bloc of the landowning class, coupled with the British and the Sultan, were able to fully preserve a favored economic position. Moreover the power bloc further entrenched and extended their social conditions of accessibility and control.

Despite majority landownership landowners could not assert economic dominance following abolition. As capitalism became more fully invested in the islands', the merchant class began to assert economic dominance over landowners. Through the power bloc alliance with the British, the landowning class was able to exercise political privilege even as their socio-economic dominance disappeared. Ultimately, this alliance lacked the ethical leadership necessary to constitute hegemony; rather it should be seen as one of domination.[54] However, in order for the landowners to first obtain and secure their position within the power bloc, there must have existed prior a socio-economic position of entitlement, represented by their position as slave owners, which allowed for the power bloc to "liquidate, or to subjugate perhaps even by armed force" their subaltern functionaries.[55] Thus, in the power bloc relationship, the political privilege of the landowning class was secured, not by economic dominance, which they no longer had, but by their alliance with the British administration. This power bloc arrangement did not fulfill the requirements of hegemony as articulated by Gramsci; rather there was an absence of civil society structures and political parties, which are necessary conditions for the exercise of hegemony and counter-hegemonic actors to develop.

      Before attempting to fully employ the terms domination and hegemony, it is beneficial to understand their differences as defined by Gramsci. As Gramsci sought to articulate the circumstances in which modern Italy found itself, he first began with the concept of domination. Domination occurs when a particular social group ascends to "supremacy" over other "antagonistic groups" through its "intellectual and moral leadership", which often takes the form, in capitalist states, as political education; the supreme social group then seeks to either "liquidate or subjugate, perhaps even by armed force" other groups in order so that it can coalesce around "kindred and allied groups."[56] As such, before hegemony can come into being, there must first be "hegemonic activity even before the rise to power" within social groups.[57] The function and utilization of domination can and does occur outside of capitalist states; it is through this process that emerging capitalist (or colonial capitalist states) come to employ certain practices that can seem hegemonic, but in fact are a form of domination.

      In employing Gramsci's term "hegemony", I have drawn on the two meanings that have come to be associated with its definition as theorized by Walter L. Adamson.[58] The first meaning is best defined as constructing an alternative to the practices of repressive domination and coercion that occurs in weak and less advanced capitalist states where repression and coercion are necessary for maintaining dominance. Though hegemony takes on numerous manifestations depending upon the particular circumstances of an advanced capitalist state, it is practiced most fully by strong states where a sustained ruling class, in alliance with other classes, becomes a historic bloc within the capitalist state. In contrast, colonial states such as Zanzibar, (where hegemony is absent) must rely on repressive security measures in order to maintain order and relative peace since there has not emerged a dominant "intellectual and moral" bloc that is able to disseminate its ideology through the institutions of the Protectorate.[59] Within the strong hegemonic-formed State, there exists cleavages (civil society) wherein the subaltern is able to create associations of counter-hegemony that are not exclusive class alliances, but can also be formed around political education, social conditions, and cultural traditions.[60] This counter-hegemonic movement may, or may not achieve hegemony over another class or even within its own class; however, there still exist conditions of possibility, which allow for a dialectical dialogue to be articulated among the subaltern that is not exclusively economic-corporate.

   As such, Zanzibar constituted a weak colonial capitalist state that was transitioning from a slave state; the political and economic institutions began to extricate themselves from one another as merchants became economically dominant and landowners were awarded political representation in the colonial state. A tenant of the strong capitalist state is the ability of civil society to dually function from within the institutions of the state, while at the same time give credence and agency to those classes often excluded from the apparatuses of economic-political power. However, this does not occur in weak or emerging capitalist states since there does not yet exist within the state a fully functional hegemonic historic bloc; only within a fully formed capitalist state can hegemony actually exist. Rather, it is based on domination and acquiescence, not consent. In Zanzibar, the *shamba* and worker classes had not come to be fully formed or conscious of their class until well into the twentieth century and could not ally themselves with other classes to form a historic bloc capable of obtaining hegemony.

   The avenues of civil society did not exist through which former slaves and mainland laborers could express or obtain agency, rather they passively accepted the domination of the colonial administration as long as it did not directly run counter to their interests. Points of resistance, discussed in Section II and III, only occurred once the colonial capitalist system became more fully invested within society and class became more firmly established among landowners, the petty bourgeoisie merchants, and smallholders.

In order to understand the development of socially created categories and classes according to a hierarchy, it is necessary to untangle the economic positions of each class as they became institutionalized through certain practices of access and denial of agency. Through this, the positions of former slaves, *shamba* laborers, and emerging semi-proletarianized urban workers, first became established through the political-ethical arena, which provided movement for expression that existed in opposition to the economic position.

Economic Transition Following Abolition

Slavery was an institutionalized practice until its abolishment in 1897. The creation of a new group of free laborers creates a historical condition of a new hierarchy that becomes fully invested within particular categories of race.[61] Mainland African ex-slaves' identification rested on their association with seasonal labor practices and limited, if any, access to the institutions of the colonial government.[62]

The Sultanate slave state ensured the movement of large numbers of slaves from the mainland to Zanzibar and Pemba twice yearly for the harvesting of cloves and other cash crops. In order to ensure that the Sultanate was able to create conditions favorable to the well being of the slave owners (through taxes extracted from exports), slaves were exploited as a source of expendable labor. The subsequent abolition of slavery as an institution under the Protectorate created a cleavage through which former slaves, though denied actual landownership until the 1920s, were forced to position themselves as *shamba* workers within the confines of an export-driven cash crop economic system. Since "the poor peasants were on the borderline between a money economy and a subsistence economy...they had [to] be[en] transformed into an inexpensive reservoir of labour to facilitate capitalist accumulation."[63] The economic dominance of the landowning class collapsed as the wealth in cloves shifted from tree ownership to export markets that were controlled by merchants. Dependence upon paid labor required that the landowners could no longer extract sufficient surplus but had to pay it out in the form of wages prior to or during harvest season, even if they were forced to later sell their cloves at a loss to merchants. As the position of landowners became increasingly precarious, which was noted by British officials following abolition, the colonial administration sought to remedy, or at the very least placate this predicament by supporting them politically through their power bloc at the expense of the economically dominant merchants.[64]

Within this new system former slaves acquired squatter rights on the land they inhabited, which, though the rights were limited, they were the first opportunity for savings. The security of their squatter rights was the informal agreement between *shamba* workers and the landowner since if the landowner lost his land due to foreclosure, *shamba* workers could also be evicted from the land. It was not the wages that the landowners paid *shamba* workers that kept them on the land, but their ability to grow food crops and the freedom to sell those crops without paying land rents. As noted by Ed Ferguson: "the exploitation of unpaid family labor to produce cash crops was the fertile soil in which appeared capitalist exploitation and accumulation among" *shamba* farmers.[65] They provided landowners with labor during the harvest season and obtained limited de facto rights; squatters were able to cultivate their small settlements (usually around one to two acres) in between the clove and coconut trees in order to grow their own food crops. In exchange for land security and the freedom to grow and sell their own crops, the squatters provided landowners with directly accessible laborers whose skills were maintained throughout the year and were far more efficient than imported mainland labor. Unlike slaves, who had to be imported during harvest seasons and very often died within one year due to conditions such as disease and malnutrition (not to mention deaths as a result of climbing the tall thin clove trees), post-abolition *shamba* workers were directly tied to the land on which they harvest cloves and coconuts. Not only did this help with retaining skills each year (climbing being very important), but the *shamba* workers were cultivating and harvesting land on which they held a common interest to that of the landowner.

Once the slave-based economy transitioned to one of *shamba* workers and urban laborers who were composed of dispossessed former slaves, the utility of a class-based function became apparent to the power bloc.[66] However, the emergence of a particular class is based upon the denial of privileges assumed by and conferred upon the ruling class within the dominant power bloc; these particular privileges were created by the conditions of economics, but only realized in actuality by the power bloc that has assumed them. The position of the power bloc within the administration of the Protectorate occurred because of the economic privilege of the landowning class, but only after the introduction of the colonial capitalist system that allowed for the accumulation of profit and the security of that profit through controlled domination as exercised by the power bloc. Control of the Protectorate, though directed by the British authorities, such as the Governor General, functioned through the use of the power bloc's agents and "deputies" who sought to maintain their position through the acquiescence of the *shamba* class.[67] These agents were composed of civil servants, who were of mixed mainland origin as well as indigenous African Zanzibaris, who were employed as rent collectors, export tax agents, and most importantly the local police force. This occurred without resistance due to the dispossession and fragmented unawareness that constituted the former slaves' position within the economic, as well as socio-political structures of the islands.

Though the British functioned as a coercive security force, their ever-present ships docked in the Zanzibar Town port, repressive measures ultimately became an expensive practice by the mid-1910s. Inaugurated in its place were practices of economic necessity following abolition (hut taxation and imposition of land rents being the two most important, see pages 56-60 and 71-72) that provided, at the very least, a minimal need for employment and capital resources to obtain goods imported by the colonial state.[68] The imposition of taxation created a system of free labor that necessitated laborers to work and engage with former slave owners for low wages in exchange for free land on which they could cultivate cash crops. While there remained, at least immediately following abolition, a greater demand for labor than could be provided by the domestic population, the colonial administration enacted legal enforcements against former slaves who refused to work. This included not only the hut taxes and ground rents, but also imprisonment and deportation to the mainland. Landowners sought to retain laborers on their lands by providing them with concessions of housing, autonomy, and economic mobility through the utilization of squatter's rights.[69] However, this relationship constitutes not one of reciprocal gain since it favors the landowners who reinforce the previous practices of labor exploitation without the economic burden of sustaining a plantation of slaves each year.

Colonial Identity and State Power

Resistance to and against the power bloc did not occur in the period immediately following abolition because the organization and cooperation of the *shamba* workers and the urban wage earning classes did not exist, nor were they consciously aware of their subjugated position.[70] Political identity, as it relates to the plight of a particular group in relationship to that of other groups, did not come into being until it had been constructed and established by the power bloc. The shift from a slave-based economic system of exploitation and bondage to one of piece wage labor was not immediate, but had to be cultivated from within the Protectorate through the positions of the power bloc. The British effectively eliminated the slave owning class in order garner "support from the groups which actively or passively assisted them"[71] in the displacement of the Sultan as the ruler.

In order to successfully establish and sustain domination over urban workers and *shamba* farmers, the British found it best to continue to cooperate with Arab landowners by supporting them economically and integrating them into the political administration of the Protectorate; though this only occurred to a limited degree politically with the establishment of the Legislative Council in 1926 (discussed in Section II), it was significant for the purposed exclusion of all other classes. As had been practiced during the absolute rule of the Sultan with the settlement of Arab slave traders into plantation owners, the British sought to incorporate and protect as much as possible the class of Arab landowners using the legislative and social means of the colonial administration. Not only did this allow for the British to maintain control over the population indirectly and most efficiently, but also further extended the authority of the newly constituted power bloc over their subjects.

Establishing Domination

The exercise of hegemony functions only to the extent that it is able to balance "the combination of force and consent…without force predominating excessively over consent."[72] By utilizing landowners as economic producers, as well as elites who served as political agents in the Protectorate administration that favored landownership, the British successfully incorporated a shift from a slave-based economy to one of labor exploitation. This was necessitated by economic need of the *shamba* for a living wage in the face of private landownership and the forms of taxation imposed by the administration. Coupled with privatization was the commodification of foodstuffs and the accumulation of surplus value for urban laborers, as well as by Indian merchants, which allowed for expendable transfers of money and extensions of credit to landowners. This became further institutionalized through the practice of squatter rights, which most former slaves acquired in the decades following abolition.

Since obtaining ownership of land was out of reach financially for most former *shamba* slaves, they by-and-large acquiesced to stay on the plantations of their former masters in exchange for free housing and a plot for subsistence farming. However, implied within this relationship of exchange was the use of former slaves during harvest season for labor on the plantation, for which they also received a wage. There was markedly little difference, with the exception of wages, between the three-to-four day workweek as was employed during slavery and the work contracts that existed post-abolition. While the workers were no longer legally bound to the landowners, as they were during slavery, their wages depended upon either the length of their work, or piece-wages based upon the amount of cloves picked within a given day.

As was often the case following abolition and well into the 1920s, labor shortages were caused largely by the lack of will or desire of former slaves to employ themselves in the same work as before. Since individuals were finally freed from servitude and work obligations as a matter of life and death, they found that they did not need wages in order to provide food and shelter for themselves or their families. Though many slaves did not have poor relations with plantation owners, as could be expected they did not feel an obligation towards their former masters. The menial labor of clove picking was viewed as a slaves' job and no longer worthy of the newly self-identified Swahilis, as many former slaves took to calling themselves. The changing racial identity of emancipated slaves and their pursuit to distance the present circumstances from their past caused many to refuse the work that had for so long been forced upon them. As such it fell onto imported mainland African free laborers to fill the vacuum of dependable local labor as they were viewed as a lower class who came to work but not necessarily to live on the islands. As shown in table 1, some imported laborers did choose to reside in the islands following their labor contracts, though many returned to the mainland with their wages. Locals who did undertake employment on plantations during harvest season would ask for wages up front from the landowners, though some did so without intending to actually work thereafter. Since mainlanders could not afford to make the return voyage without their pay, which were piece-wages, they were obligated to fulfill the length of their contracts.

Table I: Mainland Labor Population: 1923-1931

Date	Mainlanders Entering	Mainlanders Leaving
1923	4,334	2,478
1924	4,233	1,740
1925	3,820	3,943
1926	5,392	2,813
1929	448	1,025
1930	790	1,071
1931	2,368	965

Source: Anthony Clayton, *The 1948 Zanzibar General Strike*, The Scandinavian Institute of African Studies, ~ Uppsala 1976:14. (Note: No figures were published for years 1927-28)

Though former slaves and agricultural laborers now found themselves incorporated within the emerging colonial capitalist structure and were allowed to sustain themselves upon actual wages and work contracts, their periods of labor were episodic and brief. The landowners established a system of domesticated labor-wage in order to obtain compliance from workers who now depended upon landowners for their well being, as well as access to housing and associated rights.

Economic policy becomes the driving force and practice of the colonial state so that profit is retained by those whose economic dominance perpetuates their authority; at the same time, in sustaining a labor force for wage-work, surplus value is created by workers and appropriated for accumulation by the landowning and merchant classes. This policy provided the foundation for the later development of a capitalist state and was necessary as Zanzibar transitioned from a slave to a capitalist state. Only by ensuring that those who administer the colonial government and economy are allowed to secure profits can the power bloc successfully retain, over time, their hierarchical position.[73]

Though economic reform, following the boycotts of the 1920s, of the Protectorate contained within it certain concessions to and for the working and agricultural classes, in return for their acquiescence, these reforms "cannot touch the essential; for though [it] is ethical-political, it must also be economic, must necessarily be based on the decisive function exercised by the leading group in the decisive nucleus of economic activity." [74] Though practical reforms, discussed in Section III, may address certain grievances, these are never instituted without first measuring not only their success of method, but also how they are able to further perpetuate the systematic renewal of agency within the ruling class at the expense of all other classes.

In coming into being, the Protectorate sought to disband the political and economic unity of the Sultan and Arab landowners in order to replace it with a divided system of rule. Classes cannot be managed through outright repression, since the amount of force that must be effectively applied for repression would outweigh the ability of the British administration to enforce such methods. Rather, by instituting practices of exclusion and privilege that are furthered by economic necessity, the British were able to separate the political ruling class from also being economically dominant. As such, hegemony could not have develop and come into being, rather domination played the crucial role in organizing and enacting the abolition of slavery and administering a new order of socio-economics. The material conditions that are marketed by the creation of surplus value, inherently produce a class who must acquire "the habits and customs necessary for the new systems of living and working, or else they continue to be subject to coercive pressure through the elementary necessities of their existence."[75] Former slaves could not be physically forced into become wage laborers, though methods were certainly instituted unsuccessfully in an attempt to put them to work. However, conditions of economic necessity, as well as the increase in the availability of commodities, brought about favorable results in creating a sustainable domestic workforce, though there continued to be resistance well into the 1900s. The loss of political authority for the Sultan and the collapsing economic dominance of Arab landowners provided an opening for the British to most effectively take control of the changing socio-economic order in the Protectorate. These significant changes would have sustainable and far-reaching impacts in the twentieth century as Zanzibar developed away from a slave state and became integrated into the British colonial capitalist enterprise.

Section II: THE FUNCTION AND CREATION OF CLASSES WITHIN THE PROTECTORATE 1897-1926

The colonial administration undertook and instituted certain measures as demanded by the changing relationship to production following the Anglo-Zanzibari War of 1896. Once economically dominant landowners immediately found themselves not only without slaves, but were also no longer in a position of political authority through their intimate relationship with the figurehead Sultan. In order to avoid upheaval, the British administrators realized it was necessary to bring landowners into alliance and place them under their protection by privileging them economically even though the landowners were no longer economically dominant. At the same time, the formation and emergence of African *shamba* smallholders, and urban workers became possible only after the abolishment of slavery, which shifted the need for laborers from one of permanently owned non-wage earning slaves, to seasonal piece-wage contract workers.

To create a localized and sustained demand for imported goods from across the British Colonial Empire, the mass majority of the population had to, in effect, be able to acquire a piece wage for their physical labor. The piece wage became the most direct process through which agricultural production could be sustained even during low periods of work availability. Once harvest season began, which typically ran August-September and December-January, the intensive work required fostered competition in order so that those workers who produced the largest amount of goods (cloves, coconuts) received wages according to amount or weight of their product. Any profit that they obtained through this work could be reinvested in their own land (though this land may not legally be the workers', but through *de facto* squatters' rights was his to do with as he wishes) where cash crops were grown for resale during the off-months of harvest in order to sustain the family unit.[76] In turn, wages came to be used to purchase imported commodities such as "cloth, sugar, and kerosene," which quickly became "basic needs" and, in effect "pull[ed] the peasantry into capitalist production relations."[77]

However, for such a class to emerge, there first had to exist a class in opposition who, through their own relations to production, control the ability and distribution of such wages. Under the Sultanate, landowners did not employ a paid labor force but rather depended upon slave laborers purchased at market. After abolition, the twice-seasonal habits of harvesting became economically prohibitive for many landowners, who were not accustomed to paying wages, notably prior to harvesting as demanded by many workers; harvesting required local labor that could be called upon quickly, but whose sources of employment post-harvest were limited, episodic, and brief. Rather, wages were introduced by the colonial state in order to inaugurate and establish small-scale capitalism on the islands. Following the abolition of slavery, the colonial state provided slave owners with "monetary compensation for property they lost in persons" in order so that they could employ their former slaves, who now were "bonded to former masters as squatters on the old estates."[78]

Since the colonial state depended upon export and import taxes for about 50 per cent of their budget, it became of primary concern for there to be enough surplus labor available on the islands for harvesting.[79] Following the abolition of slavery, many large-scale plantations that had been owned by the Sultan were divided and sold off to other landowners. While the Sultan, or rather the colonial state at this point, remained the single largest landowner in the Protectorate up until 1964, the colonial government as such was not a direct employer of workers as they were under contract with the Sultan. To create wage workers immediately following abolition, the colonial state instituted conditions of economic necessity, discussed below, in order to obtain employment of local laborers during harvest season; however, demand could not be met by the local population and immigration of mainland Africans continued to fill a crucial need for labor.

As imports came to be seen as basic necessities to nearly all Zanzibaris, the amount of imports increased accordingly, providing the colonial state with larger custom revenues. Zanzibar had been an important trading port since before the time of the Sultan Sayyid Sa'id; merchants and slave owners had long since been accustomed to purchasing goods from India, Africa, and Europe. With the introduction of wages during the colonial period, *shamba* farmers and urban laborers found themselves acquiring goods long out of their reach. In this manner, as shown in table 2, the British created the conditions necessary for imports to become a function of daily living. The significance of imports and their role in facilitating the need for wage earnings corresponds to the circumstances by which workers emerged through socio-economic influences according to historical racial categories that will be examined in this section.

Table 2: Average Annual Customs Revenue (in 1,000 Pounds Sterling)

Period	Export Duty (Value)	Export Duty (Total)	Import Duty (Value)	Import Duty (Total)
1916-20	119	35%	65	19%
1921-25	197	39%	106	21%
1926-30	132	27%	132	27%
1931-35	116	24%	131	28%
1936-40	111	23%	135	32%

Source: (Ferguson, Value Theory and Colonial Capitalism: The Case of Zanzibar 1897-1945 1989): 48.

Thus the colonial state created conditions that incubated two particular classes, one of landowners and one of wage earners, and demanded the adherence to such a policy of piece wage labor in order to further establish the reciprocal exchange in the relations of production.[80] The *shamba* workers had to be coalesced through economic demands into accepting a wage for their physical labor as they did not have a need for wages to pay ground rents, which in turn allows them to purchase material goods; or, as a good capitalist eventually realizes, to procure land for which they are able to further enrich themselves materially.

The differences in landownership between the islands of Zanzibar and Pemba are stark in their divisions of racial composition, as will be discussed in detail, and further lends legitimacy to the emergence of political parties that were not based upon racial identification, but in fact were ultimately rooted in class composition and alliances between them. This provided the power bloc with a vested interest in class relations as they developed within the political economy, while also shielding them from any direct confrontation or resistance from within the working class. In doing so, landowners became dependent upon production for survival, but refrained from undertaking the repressive measures necessary to regulate a labor force. Instead, the colonial state created conditions that were conducive to the acquiescence of urban working and *shamba* farmers to acknowledge the need for a piece wage in order to sustain itself materially. Thus, the landowners needed not rely on outright repressive measures, for which they do not have the force required to do so over the long-term; only the colonial state was able to adopt measures and methods of economic necessity through taxation that complied *shamba* to work. Dependent upon the creation of the *shamba* worker class was the domination of the landowner class whose control of landownership brings with it a form of agency that is denied to squatters. This agency of landownership was further ensconced and underscored in the favorable position that the landowners have within the Protectorate. Class and power was therefore derived not only from internal identification through economic leadership and landownership, but also from alliance to the colonial administration.

After abolition, the Protectorate needed to insulate landowners not only from the forces of the world capital market, but also from the uncontrollable factors related to poor harvests. The export of cash crops, most importantly of cloves, had come to be monopolized by a merchant class whose racial composition was pre-dominantly Indian and South East Asian. It was not without coincidence that the largest export markets for cloves were India and Indonesia. Due to this export monopoly on behalf of a handful of Indian merchants, landowners became deeply indebted to merchants on speculation of harvests, the price of which was determined not only by international markets, but also by ability of the merchant class to extract monetary concessions from landowners. The merchant class remained reluctant in foreclosing on the defaulted estates of landowners as merchants did not regard plantations ownership as profitable in comparison to their current economic position; instead they "sought security for their capital in high rates of interest and by establishing their claim directly on the crop, retaining landowners as little more than managers."[81] By claiming ownership of crops rather than the land, merchants could employ the foreclosed landowner as administrator of the estate without having to directly bear responsibility for paying wages and hiring workers. Moreover, as foreclosures became more frequent, the colonial administration sought measures, discussed below, which prohibited foreclosure of plantations nevertheless merchants maintained a strong hold on the export market and achieved far greater economic dominance than landowners.

The Decline of the Landowning Class

While they remained without political power for the first few decades of colonial rule, the merchants were able to extract concessions from landowners by laying claim not to the actual land which had become indebted to them, but to that of the physical crops. Landowners became "little more than managers" of their own estates as their profits were funneled directly to the merchant class to pay off debts.[82] Rather than foreclose upon a plantation, merchants would allow the landowner to continue to manage the estate with any profits going towards payment of the loan and the landowners receiving a wage from the merchant for his role as manager; however, since landowners required a loan each year to hire workers during harvest seasons, and had not paid off the loan from the year prior, the merchants would extend the former loan and tie it to the new loan, in effect placing landowners in perpetual debt. This became a source of concern for the British administration as they sought to ensure that only the class of "Arab" landowners maintained control of large plantations since they maintained that Zanzibar was and always would be an Arab state.[83] By protecting the Arab landowning class, the British ensured that landowners would retain their allegiance to the Sultan and the administration would be secure from unrest. This was due not to any tradition form of landownership that had been inherited from the Sultanate, but rather was due to the increasing economic domination of the merchant class and "the activities of merchant capital," which, when it "collided with the interests of advanced capitalism, it would be the latter which would prevail."[84]

An equally as important factor was Islamic inheritance laws that contributed to the decline of estates. However, this was circumvented by using the practice of turning land into *awqaaf*, which were proscribed religious trusts that were managed by the decedents of the owner in order to prohibit the further division of the land with each successive generation. In Zanzibar, the majority of the islanders followed the Shafi'i school of law, which did not allow for the transfer of the *waqf* under any circumstances. However, the minority Omani landowners, who often held the larger plantations, followed the Ibadhi law, which "allowed for the sale and exchange of *waqf* property, under particular circumstances" and was met with much more approval by the colonial state.[85] Since land increasingly became scarce and the proliferation of *waqf* prohibited parcels of land from being transferred or sold, the colonial administration set up the Waqf Commission in 1905 in order to "privatize waqf property, particularly that which produced little revenue for the Crown;" this usually occurred by declaring managers of the properties to be incompetent, and "were most often leveled against female and poor waqf managers."[86]

By creating a *waqf* landowners not only ensured that their land parcels would be held intact following their death, but would remain free from foreclosure due to debts, which was legally prohibited. Rather than directly controlling the *waqf*, since it was not directly passed down but was held in a trust or by a mosque, heirs could and did rent or lease the land in order to support themselves. According to Fair, by 1900, nearly half of the properties on Zanzibar Island were "dedicated as *waqf*."[87] In order to combat what the colonial administration viewed as a problem, the Waqf Commission approached the Sultan and asked that he impose ground rents (see Section III) in the Ng'ambo section of Zanzibar Town. The Sultan signed control over *waqf* in Ng'ambo to the Commission; as claimed by Fair, this was significant since large sections of the Ng'ambo had been dedicated as *waqf* by previous sultans to ensure that the poor, and his former slaves, would always have a place to reside without taxes or rent. By signing over rights to his *awqaaf*, the Sultan constituted a serious breach of Islamic law.[88] An overzealous romanticism of the Arab Sultanates' power over the populace became the unquestioned colonial mandate in British support of landowners.[89]

Politicalization of Racial Terms

Former slaves found it advantageous to identify themselves in the period immediately following abolition as Swahili, i.e. a costal resident. This fluid and non-descript category was founded on identification with mainland Africans; but, as scholars of the Swahili admit, there is no set definition of Swahili as a social construct other than their proximity to the coastal strip of Eastern Africa.[90] This identification was necessitated not by circumstances related to the historical racial background of former slaves, but was created due to the conditions of legitimization, as termed by British census taking officials, that were imposed upon them. The colonial administration found it in their interests to associate and sanction their agency through the apparent "external manifestation" of race.[91] The colonial state found it advantageous, as was common policy in British colonies, to articulate a hierarchical structure within society based upon observable characteristics.

The categorization of groups and individuals based upon racial factors are quickly apparent and historically conditioned according to terms created by the colonial administration and imposed upon the urban working and agricultural classes. The systematic application of racialized hierarchy by the British was enacted due to the conditions of material resources and their distribution.[92] By ensuring that former slaves retained their identification, not as slaves per se, but as socially inferior individuals whose skin color was markedly different than that of British, Arabs, and Indians, the power bloc manifested economic inequalities into those of racial inferiority. This gained further credence due to the application of European "scientific" theory (i.e. social Darwinism) which found that Africans were not only inherently weaker human beings intellectually, but were also prone to laziness and uncleanness. The latter "conditions" were viewed as most unfavorable to the requirements of the post-abolition economy based on expendable ready labor. Ultimately, the British found its leadership justified in instituting practices to develop working class habits among the urban African classes. [93]

By associating and legitimizing class hierarchy based not on the privileges of landownership, but upon justified biological factors of inferiority associated with barbarism, the power bloc was able to further extend its position in the administration of the Protectorate. The colonial state, whose membership was composed of the landowning class and the British, effectively destroyed the ability of urban workers and *shamba* farmers from constructing a dialogue of discourse. The acquiescence of these classes was fundamental to the power bloc, but could not be maintained solely through economic exploitation and disenfranchisement; instead, the colonial state justified itself as a civilizing mission and found it advantageous to expound an ideology of superiority in progressing society forward through the application of social Darwinism. Colonialism necessitated the imposition of racialized inferiority according to class relations.

The Function of the Power Bloc through Colonial Ideology

Further adding to the British definition of African "otherness" was an inherently inferior racial classification whose own feebleness required it to be regulated in order so that these individuals could be brought up to the standards of their colonial masters. This often took the form most readily through "routine health and sanitary inspections by colonialists" which not only intruded upon the lives of urban workers, but added a further "ordinariness of [colonialists] power."[94] The simplicity for such tactics of colonial rule sought to further subjugate the workers and agricultural laborers by labeling and classifying them as a group who was in need (according to the standards of the Metropole) of being observed for the betterment of themselves as a whole.

In articulating a negative conception of the urban workers and *shamba* farmers, the colonial state sought to isolate them in order so that the former would be unable to obtain access to cleavages of an emerging civil society. Furthermore, in framing the African classes through negative socio-political terms, the British successfully separated out the true circumstances of inferiority, their class.

Within less than a generation after post-abolition, former slaves found themselves in a position through which it became possible, socio-economically, and politically, to obtain ownership of the land from which they had so long been excluded. Two inter-related factors contributed to the final emergence of small holders of land. The first was the increasing indebtedness of the large landowners to the merchant class who had extended credit to them during the harvest season. By the 1920s, many large landowning estates could not be sustainably run for profit and went bankrupt, after which they were divided into smaller units. These small units of land, with clove and coconut trees, began to be purchased not by the merchant class, but rather by the squatters who had saved enough to be able to acquire land.[95] This forms the second factor in the emergence of a new small holder class, the ability of former slaves to utilize their land to grow cash crops that could be resold or traded at market for a profit. Since the familial unit contains within it expendable labor, *shamba* farmers were able to freely use wives and children as units of labor who could be exploited as agricultural workers upon their own small plots. In turn, they could accumulate profit from the selling of cash crops that could be harvested even while the *shamba* farmers were obliged to harvest cloves.

The inability of former slaves and mainland laborers to form a class for itself did not stem from their own disorganization, but rather was constrained by the exercise of domination by the British and landowners. They came to articulate and define themselves not according to a strict class segment; instead, they formulated a racial identity as requested, employed, and created by the British administration. Not only was racial composition used by the administration for purposes of census taking, but came to define and reinforce the landowning class structures and practices society. Though the increasing indebtedness of landowners was becoming unsustainable and undermined their alliance in the power bloc, the British continued to discriminate against *shamba* farmers, mainland laborers and urban workers through institutionalized policies and practices. The 1921 Public Lands Decree stated that "only 'native' or indigenous Zanzibaris were rightfully allowed to claim...land on which former slaves had established their homes and farms in the preceding decades...the Swahili were specifically defined as being 'non-native' for the purposes of land acquisition." [96] By securing ownership of the land for the privileged minority, the power bloc sought to retain its position of domination by excluding other classes from undertaking measures to increase their access to agency.

However, former slaves, who had adopted the label of Swahili following abolition, quickly abandoned the category and began identifying themselves as Shirazi (see below) in order to claim ownership as indigenous Zanzibaris. [97] Ownership could be obtained, but only through the methods that had been determined by the colonial state. This divided the community into Shirazi, who were native Zanzibaris, and the mainland African community who immigrated during harvest season, a portion of whom became residents of Zanzibar. The legal advantages of being classified as "native" far outweighed any actual or idealized identification of race and further entrenched a racialized hierarchy within the islands.

Resistance, Identity, and Consciousness

Rather than simply acquiescing to these socio-economic policies of subjugation, former slaves found it easier to simply classify as an all-together different race that was not systematically denied landownership. The new identification of Shirazi was presumed to facilitate two avenues of empowerment for the disaffected former slaves. The first was the mythical historical narrative that the Shirazi claimed heritage from early generations, before the arrival of the Portuguese. This community supposedly emigrated from the city of Shiraz, Persia (now Iran) and was afforded a similar, though lesser level of legal rights as Arabs. The second was that since Shirazi preceded even the Portuguese, they were most definitely classified as natives of Zanzibar and thus able to obtain access to landownership, as well as other socio-economic rights and privileges. Not only did this formulate their identification using terms created and defined by the colonial state during census taking, but came to constitute and give agency to these terms because such identification was made possible through the accumulation of landownership; as such these terms no longer held a negative value but a positive one since they came from within the class rather than being imposed upon them.[98] These definitions came to represent different meanings at various times and by capturing these markers for themselves, the Shirazi were able to compete more fully, though limited, at the socio-economic level with the landowning and merchant classes.

Once this critical identity came into being through the direct expression of racial heritage, employed solely for the purposes of obtaining land ownership and social rights, which obscured the true relationships among classes, urban workers and agricultural laborers came into existence as a socio-economic bloc. The mass of individual agents were able to distinguish themselves from those groups whose interests ran counter to their own. Before the Shirazi were able to cultivate alliances across classes, they needed to philosophically articulate a discourse that would address not only their conditions of subjugation, but also the path necessary for reform.[99] This required an elite of intellectuals who not only represented their particular class, but also were able to coherently formulate an awareness of the power that had been obtained through the procurement of land and land rights.[100]

However, the Shirazi were prevented from holding political power even as their economic might increased incrementally through smallholdings because such political institutions did not come into being until the creation of the Legislative Council in 1926:

"Laws which were issued by the Sultan as decrees and which received his assent, required the approval of the Legislative Council. In certain instances, where it was apparent that the laws being passed would affect interests other than those of the Sultan's subjects, the British resident was required to countersign them," [101]

The Legislative Council was composed of twelve seats, six were held by members elected from the colonial administration, the other six were labeled as unofficial and were nominated as representatives of the Arab Association, the South Asian Association and later the Clove Growers Association and the Land Alienation Board.[102] It was not until after World War II that the African Association was able to nominate a councilmember. Coupled with the creation of the Legislative Council were enactments of political exclusion by the power bloc against the Shirazi and African mainlanders.

The Shirazi developed along with the creation of a proto-representative political institution, but remained suppressed as Arab landowners, the dominant merchant class, and the colonial administration sought to exclude Shirazi and mainland Africans from political power. This necessitated a struggle through which the Shirazi found that they were prevented from collectively representing their group politically and being allowed to address conditions of subjugation they felt the administration was enforcing. By shifting power from one of purely economic means (which had already been facilitated by the collapse of large landowning estates) to that of political representation within the Protectorate, the landowning class was able to successfully subdue challenges to their domination. As the Shirazi acquired a larger share of smallholdings they found that their lack of voice and political exclusion forced them to unite as a collective group outside the purview of the colonial state. From this instance the political parties of the island begin to emerge according to not only economic interests, but created racial associations as well; this process would ultimately come to define post-independence Zanzibar.

Section III: THE FORMATIVE DEVELOPMENT AND FUNCTION OF POLITICAL PARTIES 1926-1945

Racial identification within the Protectorate became more deeply entrenched as class relations became divided between small-holder Shirazi Zanzibaris and African mainlanders. This was caused not only by categorical division on behalf of the colonial state, but by the growth of Shirazi smallholders whose accumulation of land and integration within the colonial capitalist system brought with it demands for political representation. African mainlanders remained piece wage laborers and were legally excluded from landownership even if they had settled in Zanzibar. In instituting the practice of divide and rule, the British administration successfully incorporated racial divisions within the political structures of the Protectorate: "Racial representation of privileged groups within the colony encouraged those groups to think in terms of racial interests, and hence divided them...in 1946 the first African member" of the Legislative Council "was appointed."[103] The onset of the world economic depression of the 1930s crippled the export industry, causing a number of smallholders, many of whom had only relatively recently come to acquire ownership, to go bankrupt. As a result, the colonial state enacted legal measures to limit the further degradation of the landowners, but which were largely unsuccessful in curbing the mounting debts; since landowners had become the sole governing partner within the Legislative Council, the integrity of its economic well-being had to be protected from threat.

Throughout the 1920s class struggle between Shirazi smallholders, poor urban tenants in the Ng'ambo, and merchant Indian landlords came to a head. By the mid-1920s most of the land and homes of residents in the Ng'ambo district of Zanzibar Town were legally declassified as *waqf* by the Waqf Commission and were now subject to ground rents. The promise and protection of a *waqf* for them and their succeeding generations by previous Sultans was broken by the colonial administration. The Waqf Commission sold the land underneath the homes to a small group of three Indian landlords, while claiming the better parcels of land for the colonial state.[104] However, as this class struggle progressed, the realization that action could in turn extract concessions from both landlords and the colonial state prompted small holders and Ng'ambo residents to unite. Building upon the successes of the urban workers, merchant landlords staged a resistance of their own in 1937[105] by appealing to importers in India to boycott cloves from Zanzibar until they succeeded in enacting reforms, however marginal, which benefitted their interests.[106] The economically weak position of the Arab landowning class came to depend solely upon their ability to articulate power through the mechanisms of the colonial state, thus remained entirely dependent upon their relationship with the British administration.

Establishment of the Political Structure

In limiting the political representation of the economically powerful merchant class, the British legitimized a constructed hierarchy that remained embedded in the confines of the urban city, Zanzibar's Stone Town, at the expense of the rural masses. To stave off the immanent dissolution of indebted landowners, the British colonists legitimized the necessity of their partner through the creation of the Legislative Council in 1926.[107] This exclusive, non-elected and non-legislative advisory council was proposed as an effective measure to counter the growing influence of not only the newly constituted Shirazi smallholders, but also that of the merchant petite-bourgeois class. Though these two classes remained unable to form an alliance between themselves, the forced exclusion of these classes from the Legislative Council initiated a further development of political consciousness within each class.

Before diverging too far into the complexities of political-class formation within Zanzibar, it is necessary to define the development of political parties through Gramscian terms:

"Clearly it will be necessary to take some account of the social group of which the party in question is the expression and the most advanced element. This history of a party, in other words, can only be the history of a particular social group. But this group is not isolated; it has friends, kindred groups, opponents, enemies…Hence it may be said that to write the history of a party means nothing less than to write the general history of a country from a monographic viewpoint, in order to highlight a particular aspect of it. A party will have had greater of less significance and weight precisely to the extent to which its particular activity has been more or less decisive in determined a country's history."[108]

The coherence of a collective will to action of a particular class has been conditioned and constructed by its socio-historical circumstances.

Relationships among other classes ultimately come to represent the interests of that class through a discourse articulated by intellectuals from within the class.[109] Though a political party is created by the conditions within a particular class, and only from within that class, the influence of other actors, both negative and positive, contribute to the development of the party. Gramsci states:

"Although every party is the expression of a social group, and of one social group only, nevertheless in certain given conditions certain parties represent a single social group precisely in so far as they exercise a balancing and arbitrating function between the interests of their group and those of other groups, and succeed in securing the development of the group which they represent with the consent and assistance of the allied groups--if not out and out with that of groups which are definitely hostile."[110]

The movement from class struggle to the development of a political party and platform is based upon the conditions that have been created according to the ruling class. In order to gain a voice and power, the marginalized classes must form or align themselves into a political party.

The process of appointment was extremely limited due to landownership restrictions and was done in consultation with the Sultan and the British Resident. Only representatives who were most favored by the elite class of landowners would be selected. The founding of the Legislative Council for political control was followed by the creation of the Zanzibar and Pemba Clove Growers Association (ZPCGA) by the colonial administration in April 1927 in order to strengthen the economic stability of landowners by "of gaining control of the total clove market, of regulating plantation costs by fixing labourers wages, and of securing funds for a systematic regeneration of clove estates."[111] The creation of these two institutions indicated a centralization of power in appropriating political and economic control.

It is not by coincidence that the only class, Arab landowners, to be allowed into the political apparatus of the Protectorate was the same class whose influence was far greater than its economic means. Rather, the landowners capacity for power, invested through their alliance with the British, extended across socio-economic boundaries. The Protectorate came to function according to the dictates of the British, in favor of landowners, and was not representative of the interests of the masses. The function of the ruling class was to "disintegrate" and "detach" all other political parties from their base so as to achieve control within the political institutions of the colonial state.[112] The landowning class felt itself increasingly threatened by the growing number of small holders who were achieving economic independence. The large increase in the Arab population, see table 3, from 1924-1948 corresponded more to individual identification as Arab for purposes of rationing during World War II (see Section IV), as well as landownership laws that favored non-Africans, than it did to a natural increase in Arab births and migration.

Table 3

Population of the Arab Community: 1924-1948

Census	1924	1931	1948
	Population	Population	Population
Arabs	18,884; 8.7%	33,401; 14.2%	44,560; 16.9%

Source: Michael F. Lofchie *Zanzibar: Background to Revolution.* Princeton: Princeton University Press, 1965: 74.

At this juncture, the cleavages of civil society are not yet fully established and must undergo a period of incubation before they are structures conducive to counter-hegemonic development. However, civil society associations became more fully formed as the economic conditions of the Arab landowners deteriorated further and the Shirazi, along with Indian merchants, were able to slowly overtake the means of production through acquisition of landownership. By the late 1920s, semi-proletarianized urban workers, *shamba* farmers, and Indian merchants, had transformed social relations of production in the Protectorate from a slave-based society to one of free labor and colonial capitalism.

Communal Associations, The Birth of Civil Society

Though civil society institutions are often weak or non-existent in pre-capitalist societies, the development of colonial capitalism provides the unique opportunity for limited alliances of workers within the classes excluded from Legislative Council.[113] Civil associations started simply as a football team or dance group within the communities of Ng'ambo and the countryside of Zanzibar and Pemba; eventually they developed into trade unions that came to represent the class of urban workers.[114] Football clubs had been an important and integral part of the lives of many men and by 1920 Protectorate sanctioned sports clubs had been formed by various civic departments, including "the Public Works Department (PWD), the Police, and Medical Department" that were managed by the Sports Control Board with Protectorate oversight.[115] However, the civic football clubs were no substitute for the independently run community clubs that for many were part of "larger social identities...built around their friends, neighborhoods, and leisure communities, not their jobs."[116] The approach, by the British, of incorporating workers into a club whose interests represented that of the Protectorate more than the worker's community fostered dissent of many club members.

The formation of Protectorate sanctioned clubs was mirrored in the emergence of trade unions that formed during the 1930s. The expressed intent and mandate of trade unions is for the interests of a particular class fraction, e.g. *shamba* workers and semi-proletarian laborers; the imposition of the colonial state with regulations of governance, which prohibited civil servants from joining political or trade associations, prevented trade unions from truly taking form.[117] In excluding the masses from the political and legislative processes of the colonial state, but mandating that they include themselves in Protectorate-sponsored sporting clubs and trade unions, the colonial state suppressed alternative structures of social expression.

The colonial power bloc limited itself by defining its practices according to the perceived socio-economic importance of landowners. Increasing economic opportunities and expansion of surplus value contributed to a rise in the need for political dissent and a discourse of reform. Communal associations spread "increasingly salient elements of people's twentieth-century social identities," that formed the basis of civil society.[118] The expansion of community associations, along with increased accessibility of landownership, led to awareness of political exclusion on behalf of the African mainlander and Shirazi communities. The increase in Shirazis' acquiring land that had been previously owned by Arab landowners contributed greatly to the separation of African identity into two distinct categories, mainlanders and natives. By the 1930s the Shirazi landowners had come to identify themselves increasingly with the economic interests of the decaying Arab landowners.

The development of racial identification for purposes of social and political empowerment, such as the fluid category of Shirazi, allowed former slaves to distance themselves from negative historical connotations. Due to the increasing bankruptcy of large plantations, which had never been designated as *waqf*, *shamba* workers began to acquire small plots of land from these plantations using capital they had gained through the selling of cash crops using household labor.[119] The Land Protection (Debt Settlement) Decree of 1938, as well as the Land Alienation Decree of 1939, placed severe restrictions of the sale and foreclosure of large plantations. Under the former decree, the government in effect took over debts of farmers and landowners while the latter decree ensured that "a seller of land 'must always keep sufficient property for the proper maintenance of himself and his dependents."[120] This effectively ended the practice of leveraging the mortgage of plantations to cover the expenses of harvesting cloves with the government becoming the ultimate lender of capital for landowners. This ensured that the landowners maintained control of their estates for the time being, even as their economic base erroded and the power of the merchant class increased. Though legal foreclosures ceased, the colonial administration did nothing to address the actual problem of landowner indebtedness and their reliance on merchants for loans to pay wages.

The decrease in large estates correlated to an increase in the ownership of small family-run holdings by the Shirazi. With the passage of the Land Protection and Land Alienation Decrees the British effectively forbade the acquisition of large estates by prohibiting their foreclosure due to debts. The authority of the landowning class became increasingly undermined through these decrees that were meant to stave off their collapse, but only further entrenched their reliance on merchant capital. The lack of profitability in large plantations, which depended upon contract wage laborers and merchants for clove exporting, remained unresolved with the decrees; the money lending practices of the merchants continued unabated.

Economic Development of the Shirazi and their Resistance

As economic empowerment became an increasingly important marker of identification, *shamba* farmers and urban workers became hungry consumers as they obtained land ownership. The ability to extract surplus value through the use of their physical labor developed more fully into small-scale capitalist exploitation of the family. As ownership of small-scale estates increased the rights of squatters became legitimized by the colonial state due to the development of growing cash crops not for consumption, but for the purpose of profit. The agricultural laborer was normally limited to brief piece wages during harvest season and long periods of unemployment in between. By utilizing members of the familial unit, wives and children, the *shamba* laborer could employ his piece wages into buying seeds to grow crops that in turn could be resold at market for a profit.[121] The increase in conspicuous consumption, the mass distribution of piece wages, and the availability of small landowning plots allowed for many families to raise their standards of living. Since employing family members as workers required no wages and limited oversight, the laborer increased the potentiality of his plot(s). No longer was the laborer subject to the regulations of the landowner because he had himself become a landowner.

Interestingly, the ownership of small estates owned by Shirazi became most fully and evenly developed on the island of Pemba.[122] The reasons for this are two-fold and dependent upon one another. First, the concentration of landowners in the Stone Town section of Zanzibar Town on Zanzibar (Unguja), prevented them from exercising much authority and control on Pemba. Moreover, the population of Pemba was spread evenly over the island in small communities and was largely devoid of urban towns or cities, unlike on Unguja. This allowed for the rural population to maintain a degree of autonomy independent from the colonial government. Previous traditions of intermarriage and communal alliances on Pemba were preserved after the establishment of the Protectorate. A history of "intermingling of Arab and Shirazi plantation owners" since the time of the Sultan contributed to the later formation of a class alliance between the Zanzibar Nationalist Party (ZNP) and the Zanzibar and Pemba People's Party (ZPPP) that negated racial associations in favor of economic interests.[123]

Since racial identification circumvented colonial state policies on ownership, Shirazi peasants came to own roughly half of all the clove plantations on Pemba by the 1920s.[124] Though these plantations were small when compared to those of the landowners on Zanzibar, they were far from insignificant. It is not without coincidence that landowning Shirazi broke from the African Association to form the Shirazi Association in the 1939, a precursor to their political party: the ZPPP.[125]

As the economic mobility of the Shirazi smallholders increased, their identification within a particular mandated racial group became one of economic convenience. It was "the concept of Shirazi" that came "to embrace all three original African tribes of Zanzibar and Pemba: the Hadimu, the Tumbatu and the Pemba."[126] By 1931, see table four, over eighty per cent of smallholdings had been acquired by the Shirazi; however, large estates remained overwhelming in the hands of a small group of Arab landowners even though they were not profitable. The cohesive unity of the Shirazi allowed for them to formulate a collective will into a fully articulate plan for action. Though the formation of definitive political party was not immediate, class unity did allow for a war of movement to be developed and directly contributed to the establishment of a party. The smallholders remained unable to fully "distinguish itself" until it had collectively "organis[ed] itself" through a class as articulated by intellectuals.[127] Through collective action, they were able to act in unity against the domination of the power bloc. The first test of collective action was the strike[128] of tenants in the Ng'ambo[129] district of Zanzibar Town beginning in 1927 by a few tenants and ultimately becoming fully established by March of 1928.[130]

Table 4: 1931 Government Survey of Land Ownership

No. of Trees on Plantations	Arab Owners	African Owners (including Shirazi)	Arabs as Per Cent of Total
1,000 & over	177	8	95.7
500-999	169	28	85.7
300-499	213	67	76.1
200-299	178	101	63.8
100-199	381	325	54.0
0-99	1,236	5,880	17.4

Source: Michael F. Lofchie *Zanzibar: Background to Revolution.* Princeton: Princeton University Press, 1965:85

Zanzibar Town, during the Protectorate, was classified into two areas roughly bisected by a creek. On a peninsula closest to the sea stood the area known as Stone Town. This area, so named for the unique stone houses that were built there, contained the Sultan's palace, as well as colonial administrative buildings and embassies. It was also where the majority of the wealthy Arab population lived. "The 1929 Building Rules established a legal separation between two halves of the city. Stone Town legally became the only 'Town' in the Protectorate; Ng'ambo was now one of a multitude of 'Native Locations'."[131] Across the creek, more inland, was a large area known as Ng'ambo, or "other side". This area grew exponentially during the colonial period, as the sultans had decreed much of the area as *aqwaaf* for the establishment of housing for former slaves in his service as compensation for their duties; this area was home to the majority of the population of Zanzibar Town. The peasants who inhabited this area often maintained smaller plots of land outside of the city or were dependent upon work in the city, which often paid higher wages than in the countryside. The lack of urban planning was a constant source of friction between the Health Administration of the colonial government, who viewed the area as full of disease and lacked proper sanitation, while Ng'ambo residents viewed incursions by the colonial state as a violation of their autonomy.

The ground rent strike of 1928 was a collective action of unity by the urban working class. It is hardly surprising, but well worth noting, that the first act of sustained resistance occurred in the main urban area of the Protectorate. The acute awareness that the Shirazi had of their subordinate position was made all the more apparent in an urban setting. Limited economic mobility and access to land meant that many of the residents in Ng'ambo were agricultural day laborers and workers who were unable to benefit from the increased landownership laborers and smallholders in Pemba experienced. Moreover, the residents of Ng'ambo were further constrained by their obligation to pay ground rents. Enforcement of rent collection was carried out not only through harsh treatment, but tenants were subject to judicial rulings seeking their imprisonment and eviction. The rights of the landlords superseded that of their tenants and were sanctioned by the colonial state. The colonial administration sought to enforce ground rents as the Indian landlords represented a strong source of economic power, as well as political presence in the Legislative Council.

Colonial State Economic Institutions and Policies

Since the single most important economic factor in the Protectorate were cloves, representation and influence within the Zanzibar and Pemba Clove Growers Association (ZPCGA) was of prime importance for landowners, small holders, and merchants. Created in April 1927, under the auspice of uniting planters, it was "represented by twenty-five districts committees in Pemba and nine in Zanzibar, each with its own president and elected council...11,000 [members] in 1928.[132] However, by the early 1930s, the ZPCGA, according to the British Resident, had come to be little more than "a purely governmental organization, but one which, by its lack of compulsory controls over the clove industry, had little impact."[133] In July of 1934 it was reorganized as the Clove Growers Association (CGA), funded directly by the colonial administration; it was invested with "the authority to purchase cloves, with the expectation of its control of large stocks of the spice ensuring a steady price, thus ending speculation," which had long contributed to the indebtedness of landlords.[134] The officers of the CGA were directly appointed by the British Resident and given direct control over the clove market. This cartel ensured that large plantations would remain insulated from fluctuations in the price of cloves on the world market with the colonial state covering any losses. The colonial state came to subsidize indebted landowners at the expense of smallholders and, above all, merchants, whose monopoly on clove exports was quashed by the creation of the CGA.

The immediate consequences of the power of the ZPCGA led to the creation of racial associations that sought to articulate the demands of their respective communities since each community (Arab, Indian, and Shirazi) were represented in the ZPCGA according to district. The Arab Association was founded around 1915 and "was dominated by the aristocratic plantation owner class."[135] Formed a decade later was the Indian National Association, which represented the interests of the largely Asian merchant class. The African Association, founded in 1934, was composed largely of mainland Africans, who maintained that "native" Shirazi could not truly speak for the African population. The African Association split in 1939 with the Shirazi forming their own association and mainland Africans comprising the remains of the African Association. As discussed, the class disparity between small-scale landowners in Pemba, who identified as Shirazi, and agricultural laborers in Zanzibar, who identified as African, contributed to the weakening of an African identity in order to obtain economic mobility and empowerment.

The demands of these associations were couched in economic terms with the leadership of these associations dominated by the most powerful economic actors within each community. However, the ultimate power and authority of the ZPCGA was to protect the interests of the landowning class. They ensured that large landowners maintained their plantations, in the hope that this would slow their deteriorating economic conditions.[136] At the same time, this alienated the economically dominant, but politically weak merchant class whose source of income came under direct control of the CGA rather than the market.

The economic vitality of the merchant class was threatened by action of the landowners, vis-à-vis the Legislative Council, in 1937 that required merchants to "purchase all cloves for export from the CGA at a price determined by the Association."[137] This culminated in a boycott of the CGA in 1937 by merchants who cut off access to the second largest clove market, India. Since the merchant class was constrained in their ability to formulate a political platform against the colonial state, due to the allegiance between the British and landowners, merchants maneuvered themselves into collective action against the CGA through boycott. The political power of the merchant class quickly became apparent as Indian importers coalesced around their brethren and refused to purchase cloves from the CGA.

The ability of the merchant class to undermine both landowners and the CGA became a moment of action for the merchants in their war of movement (see below). Twice in a decade, the urban working class and the merchant class, the former being without access to political representation, made demands against the colonial state and in both instances they succeeded in extracting concessions from the power bloc. Though the British administration largely favored landowners, they ultimately required the continual support of merchants to ensure that access to global markets, i.e. India, remained open. Any blockage or damage to the export trade had devastating consequences for the economy; as merchants began to leverage their important and strategic economic position, they realized that they wielded great power that could be used to obtain their demands. However, since the merchant and urban working classes remained economically different from one another, they did not form an alliance that could have constituted a counter-hegemonic movement.[138] Instead, both classes remained politically motivated by their respective economic interests.

The ground rent strike and boycott of the CGA are profound instances of the Gramscian term: war of movement.[139] In order to define war of movement, it is necessary to look at its counter-opposite, war of position. A war of movement is one that is waged in direct confrontation with dominant actors and attempts to destroy their position of authority. In contrast to the war of position, a war of movement does not require or utilize any apparatus of civil society since in weakened states civil society is either entirely absent or unable to be of a functional value. Though a war of position can and often does become a war of movement, it is most often employed in developed capitalist states with a strong civil society that has direct influence within the functions of a state.

In contrast to the war of position, a war of movement is similar to that of a military war of attrition, in which the subaltern must directly confront the state because civil society is either weak or is not a viable vehicle for mounting hegemony. Furthermore, such a weak state often does not have a hegemonic power bloc, but rather an autocratic or dominant power bloc that rules either through acquiescence or coercion. Gramsci attributes a war of movement to the circumstances of Russia in 1917 and the war of position to Western European states following industrialization.

By forcibly resisting the domination of the colonial state and the authority of the CGA, the merchant class was able to extract concessions from Arab landowners and the colonial administration. This war of movement was a decisively political confrontation of merchants against the power bloc. Contributing to this was the collapsing economic conditions of the British during World War II and their dependency on the economically dominant class of Indian merchants to increasingly handle the affairs of this small colony. The CGA boycott saw a compromise that appeased the merchants, but also allowed for plantation owners to sustain themselves according to Protectorate mandated minimum prices.[140]

In the case of the urban ground rent strike, the colonial state ultimately enacted a decree in November 1928 that ran counter to the interest of landlords and forced concessions from them by effectively lowering and stabilizing rents to levels not seen since the early 1900s.[141] This initial victory by the urban workers provided them with the opportunity to further develop themselves into a cohesive class that would ultimately form a political party.

While the actual formation of political parties in Zanzibar was a rather slow progression from 1926 onwards, episodic bouts of resistance and violence grew increasingly during the same period. These flashpoints centered on socio-economic tensions that continued to be further exacerbated by the increasing solidity of class factions into racial associations. The politicalization of race within the Protectorate was reinforced through the relationship inherent in the institutions and practices of colonial state. Due to conditions within which the marginalized workers and laborers finds themselves, they ultimately remained unable to fully constitute themselves into a political party until they have achieved significant progress through the war of movement. Rather, they must continually fight inch-by-inch in order to obtain rights and concessions from the British and their weakening landowning collaborators.[142]

Section IV: ZANZIBAR DURING THE TIME OF POLITICS AND THE ONSET OF REVOLUTION 1945-1964

The developments that led to the formation of race-based associations accelerated during the onset of World War II and ushered in what was known in the Protectorate as "the time of politics." While economic, social, and political tensions had all played out during the preceding decades through strikes and boycotts, it was not until conditions created by the scarcity of commodities and food during World War II (known as "the era of getting rice by ration cards" to Zanzibaris)[143] that these tensions became political flashpoints. Coupled with the difficulties of wartime rationing, the move towards decolonization on the African mainland had a profound impact on the development of nationalist ideology among the landowning class. Unsurprisingly, the first leaders to articulate a nationalist movement to free themselves from the yoke of colonial domination were the intellectuals within the Arab Association. While this may seem odd considering the consequences of divorcing themselves from their half-century alliance with the British, it is in fact a direct result of the conditions the landowning class faced as they foresaw their post-independence future.[144]

The Arab landowners realized early on that a representative parliament would signal the end of their privileged position as the majority of the population would vote according to the racial associations that had for so long articulated by the British. These tensions became deeply entrenched with the practices initiated by the colonial administration during the war years and fostered divisions between the Shirazi and mainland Africans that would be nearly impossible to heal unless drastic measures were taken. Arab intellectuals decided, rightfully so, that their only way to ensure post-independence survival was to attempt to reverse the practices of racial division created by the British and incorporate a party whose appeal would transcend racial, as well as class differences.[145]

Though the Arab landowners had faced resistance by Shirazi smallholders and urban workers, as well as the economically dominant but politically restricted merchant class, its role in institutions within the Protectorate remained largely unchanged until 1945. The appropriation of resources and the allotment of food rations served as a catalyst in creating the necessary conditions for politically excluded classes to coalesce around a central ideology stemming from within their class. Beginning with the imposition of colored ration cards in 1941, the colonial administration sought to allocate food resources towards those with the most political power according to the hierarchical structure they had created.[146] Arabs and the British classes received the greatest allotment of rations, followed by the Indian merchants, then the native Shirazi population, with the mainland African population receiving the smallest amount of rations. The war impacted the lives and well being of the citizens in the Protectorate, and their access to food, to the degree that they were systematically discriminated against by the colonial government due to their race. The alienation, embarrassment, discrimination, and ultimately, hunger, that all non-Arab groups faced during the war years helped to facilitate a discourse of resistance that could only be challenged through a political movement.

The limited ability of the Shirazi and mainlanders to politically articulate their demands led many Africans to distance themselves from the historically constructed racial categories. As noted by Laura Fair:

"Although the majority of those who lived in urban Zanzibar were excluded from formal participation in the political institutions of the colonial state, they were nonetheless actively involved in formulating the debates that constituted civil society...attempts to ascertain the economic, political, and social goals of the islands' underclass were rarely undertaken by members of the new colonial administration."[147]

While legislative decrees of economic discrimination against African landownership had led many to identify themselves as Shirazi, the pain and suffering that the community experienced during the rationing years greatly increased mainlanders identification as Shirazi since it meant greater food allotments. The Shirazi Association greatly expanded its membership as "many island residents began to perceive new and perhaps immediate material benefits from taking out a membership card."[148] At the same time, many mainland Africans and urban workers remained indifferent to the privileges attached with the Shirazi identity and remained members of the African Association. As much as the practice of rationing rice and other food staples increased divisions within the already fragmented communities, it also provided opportunities for fostering civil society organizations.

Avenues for Agency in Response to Food Rationing

The inability of the agricultural and urban working classes to articulate themselves politically, since the only avenue for political power was in the institution of the Legislative Council, forced them to explore and expand other avenues in order to express their grievances. Whether these associations were *taarb* dance clubs or football sports clubs such as African Sport and Arab Sports (for women and men respectively), or organizations formed around civil service departments, the largest being the Public Works Department (PWD), these allowed for the localized kinship relationships to become important linkages in an expanding social network.[149]

These local associations of football and dance clubs, outside the purview of the administration, provided not only an outlet for leisure activities, through which individuals could discuss the problems of their day-to-day life, but established networks through which unrelated kinship or neighborhood groups shared a common identity. Through these networks individuals could be assisted "in help finding a job, marketing one's produce, or negotiating marriage for one's child, friendships men made through these [football] teams lasted a lifetime."[150] Moreover, many women's organizations also aided its members in "the organization of weddings and funerals by helping to cook, clean, and prepare accommodations for the numerous guests who regularly attended such ceremonies."[151] Class differences that had become racialized through the racial categorization of the population became further enmeshed with the hierarchical distribution of rations. By assisting the less fortunate members of the urban community and sharing resources, these associations became the strongest source of independent agency for the urban workers.

The landowning class employed their power within the colonial state to ensure that they would receive the largest share and first access to rations. This initiated a stark shift from the relationship that had previously existed between Africans and Arab landowners for nearly two hundred years. The privileges of the landowning class had not depended upon their economic status since the abolition of slavery. Rather, their alliance with the British was based upon the ability of the British to enforce a system of domination. Once the African classes of Shirazi and mainlanders were able to foster their own collective action independent from the civic associations and ration restrictions of the colonial state, they could articulate action based on their immediate needs.

Table 5: 1948 Baston Survey of Land Ownership

Number of Trees	Arabs	Asians	All Africans	Total
3,000 trees or more	165	75		240
1,000 to 2,999 trees	320	35	215	570
250 to 999 trees	1,885	190	1,690	3,765
50 to 249	1,990	35	11,675	13,700
0 to 49	1,640	10	8,600	10,250

Source: Michael F. Lofchie *Zanzibar: Background to Revolution*. Princeton: Princeton University Press, 1965: 87

In Gramscian terms, this was the beginning of a "crisis of authority" for landowners.[152] Though their economic power had long since been overtaken by that of the merchant class, the landowning class still maintained socio-political power within the Protectorate through their alliance in the power bloc and appointment in the Legislative Council. As the Shirazi and Africans Associations marshaled themselves into community organizations, intellectuals articulated a demand for political representation within the Protectorate. As shown in table 5, there had been a sharp increase in the amount of smallholders since before the war, yet the Shirazi had still not acquired full political rights. Their demands would not be met until the first elections for a parliament were held in 1957. However, the African Association refrained from calling for the independence of Zanzibar until the 1960s due to the fear that a postcolonial Zanzibar would be ruled by the Arab minority, still viewed as former slave owners, and they would utilize their political power against the African majority.

The Emergence and Political Development of Nationalism

In 1946, the Legislative Council was reformed in order to allow two non-voting African (Shirazi) members to be appointed, bringing the total number of unofficial seats to seven.[153] Indians had been appointed to the council since 1935; however, these members were nominated by the Sultan and approved by the British Resident rather than elected through franchise. A reform enacted in 1948 allowed for the direct election through limited franchise of representatives of the Arab and Asian communities, rather than by appointment.[154] Franchise was limited to male landowners with property valued at more than one-hundred and fifty-pounds sterling or with annual incomes over seventy-five pounds sterling.[155] It was not until 1956 that franchise for African representatives was extended to the populace. No longer could Arab landowners depend upon an appointed ally in the Legislative Council but instead had to accede to the demands of the larger community, many of whom did not own large plantations and whose allegiance could sway from that of race to class. As such, the need for political parties became of paramount importance to Arab landowners. Though elections and the formation of political parties would take time to develop, Arab landowners quickly organized themselves into a political front so as to gain the upper hand. The 1948 General Strike by African dockworkers from the mainland further escalated tensions with the colonial administration.[156]

As shown in tables three and four, Clayton choose to ignore racial categories such as Shirazi in his charts because tensions during the 1948 general strike derived from differences between two groups of Africans based on wage differences related to an individual and his association as either indigenous Shirazi or as an imported mainlander.

Tables 6 & 7: African Population Composition 1924-1948

Background	1924	1931	1948
Indigenous	68,385	no figures published	81,150
Mainlander	38,590	44,492	37,404

Source: Anthony Clayton, *The 1948 Zanzibar General Strike*, The Scandinavian Institute of African Studies, Uppsala 1976:19

1924 Population Composition	Zanzibar	Pemba
Indigenous	68,385	50,977
Mainlander	38,590	26,238

Source: Anthony Clayton, *The 1948 Zanzibar General Strike*, The Scandinavian Institute of African Studies, Uppsala 1976: 44

Beginning on August 20 and lasting until September 13, the dockworkers strike represented the first sustained action by mainland Africans, who were the majority of employees at the docks, in response to their marginalized economic position.[157] Two days prior to the strike dockworkers had sent a letter to the Wharfage Company, a British subsidiary, demanding an increase of wages, "plus a free daily meal and free medical attention, and an increase in overtime rates from 25 cents to 75 cents per hour with the normal daily hours of work reduced from nine hours to eight."[158] Strikes in Mombasa in 1946 and in Dar-es-Salaam in 1947 by dockworkers had been resolved in favor of the workers with most of their demands met. This was well known to dockworkers in Zanzibar and they did not deem it unreasonable to extract concessions as had occurred on the mainland.

Within a week, three British merchant ships had been turned away from port, along with an Italian cruise liner with a reported 32 cases of typhoid who were in desperate need of medical supplies.[159] The loss of revenue from exports, which were sitting by the dockside, had an immediate effect on the British Resident and spurred him to action in order to resolve the impasse as quickly as possible. As the strike moved into September, it began to grow with employees from the Public Works Department (PWD) transport division joining in solidarity with the dockworkers. As staged demonstrations began to develop into spontaneous action, the Legislative Council passed an Emergency Powers Decree on September 6 broadly extending its policing powers and right to detain strikers.[160] After another week of negotiations, the Wharfage Company agreed to pay increases, daily meals, and increased overtime pay, though work days were still nine hours; this was accepted by the dockworkers, who "had had no pay since mid-August and many were short of money."[161] By September 13 dock and other city workers had returned to their posts with their demands largely, though not fully met.

The divisions within the African community, between mainlanders and Shirazis, increased after the war as the Shirazis' viewed themselves as socially and economically superior to the mainlanders. Recently arrived mainlanders often filled positions that the Shirazi community viewed as beneath their status. As the Shirazi had become economically mobile and came to view themselves as natives of "Persian" origin, at least for as long as it suited them economically, they no longer shared a class association with the African mainland laborers.[162] On Pemba, the Shirazi community "had an equal share of clove ownership and thus constituted a large portion of landowners," more closely aligning their interests to that of the Arab landowners than to mainlanders and urban workers.[163] This would provide a platform for an alliance between Arab landowners and the Shirazi during elections in the 1950s and 1960s. The division of the African community further reinforces the argument that racial associations were not uniform and that class played a much more important role in an individuals' identification with a particular group. This played out more fully during the late 1950s as the electoral process was initiated and political parties were forced to choose between appealing to voters' racial identification or their class status.

Table 8: Population of Ethnic Communities in 1948

Community	Zanzibar Total Number & Per Cent	Pemba Total Number & Per Cent	Protectorate Total Number & Per Cent
Shirazi	81,150; 61.2	67,330; 60.2	148,480; 60.8
African	37,502; 28.3	13,878; 12.4	51,380; 21.0
Arab	13,977; 10.5	30,583; 27.4	44,560; 18.2
Total	132,529; 100.0	111,791; 100.0	244,420; 100.0

Source: Michael F. Lofchie, Zanzibar: Background to Revolution. (Princeton: Princeton University Press, 1965), 251.

Even before the various racial associations developed themselves into political parties prior to elections in 1957, the banner of Zanzibari nationalism began to take hold through the actions of the Arab Association. Arab landowners realized that their partnership with the British during the ration years had severely damaged their relationship with the merchant and Shirazi classes as they witnessed the upheavals of decolonization on the mainland. Rather than attempt to restore their collapsing power base, Arab landowners reorganized themselves under the rallying cry for an independent, democratically elected Zanzibar. Ostensibly, this was because the landowners no longer wanted wished to remain in partnership with the domination of the British and their racially dividing practices.

Arab landowners no longer maintained economic power within the Protectorate and had become a decaying aristocracy, the majority of which were little better off than most *shamba* farmers by the 1950s. Not only had the merchant class stripped them of their economic well-being, but the increasing status of Shirazi smallholders were proving to be an economically powerful force that were becoming politically active. If democratic elections were to provide the vehicle through which the post-independent government would be formed, Arab landowners had to avoid becoming a minority and marginalized community within the majority African population. However, to limit the ability of the political parties to gather strength within the Protectorate, the British administration had issued "a special circular in 1953, which forbade any civil servants from engaging in political activity."[164] Since the majority of civil servants within the Protectorate were African, this severed any prospective alliance between them and Arab landowners.

In order to maintain their privileged social position, Arab landowners had to not only divorce themselves from their power bloc partnership, but also realign themselves with another class.[165] To do this, landowners strongly articulated the demands for an independent nationalist Zanzibar that incorporated all racial communities within the government.[166] The first action the landowners undertook was the boycott of the Legislative Council from 1954 to 1955. They demanded "universal adult suffrage, a common-roll election, an unofficial majority of elected members in LEGCO (Legislative Council), and a ministerial system."[167] Though universal suffrage was not within the interests of the landowners, they "could have been motivated by a desire to perpetuate a social structure in which a large portion of the Arab community occupied a decidedly advantageous position, especially with respect to land ownership, commerce, and government employment."[168] After eighteen months, these demands were not met; however, landowners did extract concessions from the Legislative Council that it would move forward towards independence and increase voter franchise. The Legislative Council decreed that out of the twelve unofficial members of the council, six would be directly chosen through elections based upon male suffrage, though this was limited to property owners or persons over the age of twenty-five who met certain educational requirements.[169]

By December 1955, the Zanzibar Nationalist Party (ZNP) had been formed and claimed to represent the interests of all Zanzibari citizens in the claim for independence.[170] Though the ZNP did not develop directly from within the Arab Association "its most powerful leader was an Arab, Sheikh Ali Muhsin Barwani, a member of a long-established and highly regarded landowning family of great wealth."[171] The ZNP represented the interests of the landowning class and was ultimately directly associated with and influenced by the Arab landowning class; attempts to shake off identification with the privileged landowning class greatly affected the ability of the ZNP to appeal to the majority of the population. While ZNP attempted to negate all racial and class ties, the British perceived them as a security threat that could prove hostile to the administration and sought to undermine any potential victory in the scheduled 1957 elections. The alienated African majority found their access to political agency stymied by the power bloc of the British and Arab landowners. Due to this, Africans perceived that Arab landowners had once again utilized their alliance with the British in order to marginalize the ability of Africans to unite in political opposition to the power bloc.

While the economic interests of mainland Africans and urban wage workers were contrasted to those of Shirazi landowners, they forged an alliance in 1956. The Shirazi and African Associations came to realize that the commonality of their racial marginalization was a tactic employed by the power bloc to ensure that they would be unable to unite together as a force in the upcoming election of 1957. As a result, the Afro-Shirazi Union (ASU) was formed in 1956, but with reservations on behalf of Shirazi members who felt that the party should be based on non-racial issues and instead focus upon political independence. Ideologically, Shirazi members were closer to that of the ZNP in seeking to unite the islands together in a push for independence, while mainland Africans continued to harbor negative race-based grievances. However, in February 1957 leadership of the respective African and Shirazi Associations agreed to an alliance for the purpose of the upcoming election in July, but that each respective "association would retain its separate identity" and that the two associations would be officially recognized within the ASU. [172] Though this alliance cut across boundaries of class and constructed identities of African racial heritage, it proved to be half-hearted and temporary at best as the particular economic interests could not be reconciled with the need to overcome racial divisions.

However, this alliance proved to be strong enough as the results of the July 1957 elections were tallied. Even though the electorate was limited to only males who met strict land and educational requirements, the ASU succeeded in obtaining over sixty per cent of the votes and five out of six elected seats on the Legislative Council; out of a total of twelve seats on the Council only six were elected.[173] The ZNP meanwhile suffered a humiliating defeat as not one of their candidates won a seat on the Legislative Council. The last seat went to an independent candidate from Stone Town, which was an overwhelmingly Arab district, who ran with support from the

Muslim Association. Though, as shown in table 9, he did not win the largest share of votes overall in the election, he won the district of Stone Town. Ultimately, he aligned himself with the ZNP. This circumstance was most unusual since the limited electorate should have favored more strongly the landowning ZNP party over the ASU. The failure of the ZNP allowed them to develop a more coherent, multi-racial approach toward electoral politics in favor of immediate nationalist independence, rather than the gradual process of decolonization favored by the ASU.[174]

Table 9: 1957 Election Results for the Legislative Council

Party	Number of Votes	Per Cent of Votes	Number of Seats (06)
Afro-Shirazi Party (ASP)	23,940	61.14%	05
Zanzibar Nationalist Party (ZNP)	8,604	21.97%	
Muslim Association (MA)	6,612	16.89%	01

Source: Michael F. Lofchie, *Zanzibar: Background to Revolution.* (Princeton: Princeton University Press, 1965),176.

Party Development, Breakups and Alliances

While the first election of in Zanzibar's history had gone off without violence or upheaval, the aftermath proved that the Protectorate had become more firmly divided into a complex cacophony of class, trade unions, and racial associations. The tenuous alliance between the African and Shirazi Associations ultimately broke down and in December 1959 the ASU spilt into two separate parties: the Zanzibar and Pemba Peoples' Party (ZPPP) and the Afro-Shirazi Party (ASP).[175] The ZPPP garnered support solely from the rural districts of Pemba, which were mixed districts of both Africans and Arabs small holders; however as noted by Lofchie: "neither the ZNP nor the ZPPP ever won a constituency which the majority of the inhabitants were Hadimu Shirazi or mainland Africans."[176] The ASP constituency was largely based on Zanzibar and was composed of Shirazi small holders, as well as mainlanders in Ng'ambo. During this period of infighting in the ASU, the ZNP was busily shoring up support across the island irrespective of class or racial associations.

The Zanzibar Nationalist Party (ZNP) began engaging and sponsoring trade union associations from the coconut growers industry to the dockworkers union. Though many Africans remained untrustworthy of the true intentions behind the sudden engagement of ZNP with disparate groups, the alliances with trade unions provided the ZNP with "a major vehicle through which the party built up mass popular following among Africans."[177] The actions of the ZNP managed to further separate mainland Africans from the Shirazi as the ZNP continually worked to reinforce already raw tensions between the two groups. Their ability to undertake such measures was made possible by the financial support and alliance to the landowning population of the Protectorate.[178] The economic resources and limited need for actual physical work by the landowners allowed for them to devote much more energy to politicking than the Afro-Shirazi Party (ASP) party who relied more heavily on *shamba* farmers and urban workers for support, but who lacked voting rights until universal suffrage was enacted prior to the 1963 election.[179]

In order to further gain legitimacy after their defeat in 1957, the ZNP began to encourage the cultivation of nationalist intellectuals from across the Protectorate, irrespective of their class. The utility of intellectuals helped to articulate the demands and ideology of the ZNP as the party that sought to break from the colonial administration in favor of a swift and immediate capitulation to independence. The nationalist movement that the ZNP came to represent was premised largely on the Arab landowners' fear of being shut out of the government since they represented a minority percentage of the population. It was advantageous for Arabs to stake their claim in the government prior to independence so that they would be in a position of authority and not subject to reprisals from the African majority.

The Arab landowners realized that their minority position would be precarious once the British hoisted anchor and declared Zanzibar to be independent and would precipitate into a crisis of authority. As a result, the ZNP aligned themselves with the Shirazi landowners' party due to similar economic interests. This alliance between the ZNP-ZPPP succeeded in the upcoming elections. Both the ZNP and the ZPPP ultimately came to represent the interests of the landowning class. Furthermore, the alliance between the ZNP and ZPPP was facilitated by the influx of intellectuals into the ZNP.[180] This aided in attempting to obscure the previous colonial alliance that the Arab landowners remained unable to dismiss.

The Elections of 1961

The alliance of the Zanzibar Nationalist Party (ZNP)-Zanzibar and Pemba Peoples Party (ZPPP) proved to be resilient during the January 1961 elections (see table 10); however, it did not ensure a decisive outcome in favor of the ZNP-ZPPP. Each respective party had fielded a candidate in all constituencies and, as a result, a vote that would have resulted in a victory for one candidate in a ZNP-ZPPP alliance was split between the two. In such circumstances, the Afro-Shirazi Party (ASP) was able to out perform the ZNP in constituencies, mainly on Pemba, where the ZNP and ZPPP vote was evenly split.[181] Although the ASP obtained forty-three per cent of the vote, the ZNP thirty-eight per cent, and the ZPPP eighteen per cent, the allocation of seats determined by district had awarded the ASP ten seats, the ZNP nine seats, and the ZPPP three seats. In order to form a ruling coalition government, the ASP and ZNP fought for the three ZPPP seats. Perhaps unsurprisingly but with a twist of irony, two members of the ZPPP aligned with the ZNP, while the other member formed an alliance with the ASP. [182] As a result, the government reached a stalemate with each party tied at eleven seats. Fresh elections were scheduled and held in June 1961.[183]

With six months to prepare, and far greater economic resources than the opposition party, the ZNP-ZPPP won a decisive victory in the June 1961 elections. Though the ASP won with roughly 1,000 more votes than the ZNP-ZPPP, the latter claimed thirteen seats to formers' ten. The single most important factor in determining this victory was the decision by the ZNP-ZPPP to contest constituencies that they knew they could win by fielding only one candidate. Learning from the mistakes of January, the ZPPP only contested one district on Zanzibar Island, allowing the ZNP to win victories in five constituencies. On Pemba, the ZNP-ZPPP division was more evenly split, with the ZNP contesting six districts to the ZPPPs' four. As a result, ASP candidates only won two districts in Pemba, one by less than one hundred votes. Since the allotment of seats on the Legislative Council was winner takes all based on individual districts, not outright majority vote, the ASP failed to garner enough support in Pemba to retain control of the Legislative Council. The winning coalition of ZNP-ZPPP was a success in claiming the majority of seats in the Legislative Council and would continue to prove a formidable force to the ASP.

The result was disastrous for the ASP and their constituents. Many

Africans could not understand, rightly so, that though the ASP had won the election by popular vote, they had failed to obtain the majority of seats in the Legislative Council. As a result, there was widespread post-election violence between Africans and Arabs across the Protectorate, which lasted for a number of days before order could be restored.[184] The attempts to foster a multi-racial society in the run-up to independence had failed to dissolve the past seventy years of colonial domination through practices of racial division. The ZNP-ZPPP was much better funded, staffed by educated articulate intellectuals, and had attempted to bridge the racial divide in creating an alliance between the Arab and Shirazi communities. However, the alliance was based completely on economic and political interests. Both communities of landowners felt that their alliance would secure for them control of the government post-independence and allow for them to continue capitalist practices of exploitation. They earnestly prepared for the final elections, scheduled for July 1963, which would establish the post-independence government.

Table 10: Distribution of Seats in the Legislative Council January and June 1961

Party	January			June		
	Zanzibar	Pemba	Total	Zanzibar	Pemba	Total
ASP	8	2	10	8	2	10
ZNP	5	4	9	5	5	10
ZPP	0	3	3	0	3	3
Total	13	9	22	13	10	23

Source: Michael F. Lofchie, *Zanzibar: Background to Revolution* (Princeton: Princeton University Press, 1965), 203.

July 1963 Election and Its Aftermath

Though the British continued to delay announcing a timetable for when they would officially depart Zanzibar and leave it in the hands of the people, by the election of July 1963 it was rumored that the British would not be staying past January of 1964. British official Duncan Sandys, the Secretary of State for Commonwealth Relations, stated: "internal self-government could be introduced two weeks before a new general election scheduled for July 1963, but the granting of full independence must await the outcome of this election."[185] As the votes were tallied in July, it became apparent that the Zanzibar Nationalist Party (ZNP)-Zanzibar and Pemba Peoples Party (ZPPP) alliance had secured a solid and decisive victory capturing eighteen out of thirty-one seats to the Afro-Shirazi Party's (ASP) thirteen. However, once again it was apparent that though the alliance had obtained political victory, they did not secure a mandate from the majority of voters. The ASP won nearly fifty-four per cent of votes compared to forty-five per cent for the ZNP-ZPPP. Due to this, the alliance found itself in a precarious position that was far from established. For the supporters of the ASP, the alliance had failed to obtain legitimacy even though the electoral process had been fair and participatory.[186] The ZNP-ZPPP seemed to be nothing more than an attempt by Arab landowners to retain their privileges as enacted and instituted under the colonial power bloc. Since landowners could no longer depend upon the domination of the departing British authorities and their economic superiority had long since been diminished to nothing more than a brittle aristocracy, they had to co-opt Shirazi small holders into an alliance.

Table 11: Distribution of Seats in the Legislative Council-July 1963

Party	Zanzibar	Pemba	Protectorate
ASP	11	2	13
ZNP	6	6	12
ZPPP	0	6	6
Total	17	14	31

Source: Michael F. Lofchie, *Zanzibar: Background to Revolution*. (Princeton: Princeton University Press, 1965), 219.

Reliance on the British authorities as the source for security during Protectorate had made the Arab landowners fearful of reprisals and actions against them by the mainland laborers and disaffected ASP supporters. During campaigning some factions within the ASP had claimed that if the ZNP won the election they would reinstate slavery and that the African community would be deprived of property rights by the Arab landowners. Though the ZNP had expounded a message of tolerance in a multi-racial post-colonial society, its leadership felt that the post-election violence in 1961 portended future tensions that would escalate sharply after independence. As a response to these fears and the date for independence grew nearer, the ZNP administration, which had taken office by mid-August, dismissed mainland Africans from the police force and deported them back to their country of origin. The leadership justified their actions based upon the principles that mainland Africans, who were largely the supporters of the ASP, would prove more loyal to their political party than to the integrity of the independent state. Moreover, in a tactic of divide and rule, the ZNP-ZPPP alliance reinforced the tensions between Shirazi small holders and mainland Africans by emphasizing the stark economic differences that separated the landowning minority from the *shamba* farmer and urban worker majorities. However, the ability of the administration to forcibly remove mainlanders from Zanzibar proved difficult and in turn created a mass of unemployed young men with knowledge of firearm usage and combat training. These men, marked for deportation of what they considered their homeland constituted an easily maneuverable militia that was hostile to the newly elected government that they did not vote for and who distrusted them as fellow citizens.[187]

The ZNP-ZPPP was crucial in creating a sense of distrust throughout the citizenry in the months following the July 1963 election. As the ZNP-ZPPP consolidated power, they excluded the ASP opposition from key functionary positions during a time in which this could have helped to bridge the ideological and racial separation between the parties, made all the more fragmented by the tenuous security situation caused by police dismissals. The circumstances in which the alliance formed were new and inaugurated the shift towards a more modern state with electoral processes and the incorporation of civil society into the institutions of the post-colonial state. However, the crucial partner of the power bloc remained the British administration, especially in maintaining security and order. The legitimacy of the power bloc rested solely on their electoral victory, but not on a mandate by the majority of the population. As a result, within a month of the British hoisting anchor and sailing out of the port of Zanzibar Town, rebels overthrew the elected government and replaced it with the sole rule of the ASP in January 1964.

Six years of elections, debates, and shifting associations had done little to dispel the underlying economic and political tensions that resulted in the bloody Revolution in January 1964. The ASP believed that their right to self-determination had been undermined by the ZNP due to electoral politics and their previous allegiance to the British administration and ZPPP. ASP supporters, seeing their country in ZNP terms, decried the notion that Zanzibar was an Arab state, something the British had always claimed. Rather, electoral results had reinforced material interests of the minority of the population. The Arab landowners had not been economically powerful during the entire period of the Protectorate and yet, they were politically insulated from the rest of the population by the dominating presence of the British authorities. Each attempt by former slaves and mainland African laborers to organize themselves into a collective unit was met with firm resistance by the power bloc in order to keep the Protectorate divided and the population weak. Seventy-three years of practical application of economic policies by a fragile minority in collusion with foreign agents had incubated deep pockets of hatred and resentment. As the recently established postcolonial power bloc struggled to secure their newly independent state, oppositional forces began to gather in the countryside, plotting their overthrow and destruction. This force was led by the command of one man, John Okello.

Conclusion: POST-INDEPENDENT ZANZIBAR AND THE VICTORIOUS TRIUMPH OF JOHN OKELLO

The singular role of John Okello in organizing, provoking, and successfully staging a revolution in Zanzibar in January 1964, barely one month after independence, is a striking account that often is oddly placed within the context of post-independence Zanzibar. Okello was born in Uganda and did not arrive in the Protectorate until 1959 when he found work as a policeman on Pemba.[188] He was a firm and vocal supporter of African nationalism and was greatly inspired by Julius Nyerere's role in the independence of Tanganyika in December 1961. As stated in his book, after much reflection on the troubles in Zanzibar he had arrived at the conclusion in 1962, "that revolution was the only solution."[189]

Okello arrived on Zanzibar Island in 1963 and after taking up work as a painter, became Assistant Secretary General of the Zanzibar and Pemba Paint Workers Union.[190] During his tenure, he claimed to have organized and greatly increased the membership of the trade union and allied it with other unions. The degree to which his leadership facilitated the revolution was of prime importance to its outcome.[191] He successfully mobilized mainland laborers and the disaffected former police officers across the islands to rise up in revolt against the Arab and Shirazi landowners.

As described above, the repeated denial of political access for mainland Africans and the contempt with which the postcolonial government viewed them became enmeshed with material conditions. In denying political opportunities to mainlanders and urban workers, the ruling classes of the postcolonial state of small and large landowners marginalized Africans. The weak position of the ruling classes and their fragile alliance allowed for a movement to occur and eventually overthrew them in a coup d'état. The absence of the monopoly of organized legitimate violence by the postcolonial state provided Okello with a crucial condition for orchestrating a coup.

By working within the mainland African community, through the channels of civil society by way of trade unions, Okello truly embodied Gramsci's definition of "political adventurer."[192] Okello positioned himself as a revolutionary born of the mainland; he understood that the most direct route to establish agency and trust within the community was through the politico-economic structure of trade unions. Knowing that the greatest sources of antagonism rested outside of the urban city, Okello traveled through the countryside in order to shore up support, but was reserved in revealing any details of his plans. Rather, he understood that when called to act, the rural agricultural laborers would be ready and willing to overthrow the yoke of oppression that had held them down for so long. Working with youth leagues and communal organizations, he demonstrated knowledge of both the islands and its peoples. As a mainlander, he found strong support among ASP members who resented the results of the elections and who had become further marginalized in post-independent Zanzibar.

After months of planning, Okello struck early in the morning, under the cover of darkness, on January 12, 1964. Initially with only a few dozen men, Okello successfully overtook two essential police stations and the weapons depot. Soon, more and more citizens, some armed only with sticks and clubs, sprang into action. Within the span of a few hours, he had successfully captured all essential administrative and security buildings, the radio station, as well as the most symbolic building of Arab oppression and rule, the Sultans' palace. Okello's quick and decisive victory, though bloody it ultimately became, effectively ended the political power of the Arab and Shirazi ruling class.[193]

The success and speed within which the Revolution occurred underscores the fundamental weakness of the propertied ruling classes. However, the coup d'état would not have resulted in Revolution had certain particular conditions not been met prior; the single most important factor being the departure of the British whose security forces were a constant reminder to all citizens that they were ruled by a foreign power. Even when the ruling class of Arab and Shirazi landowners had succeeded in elections, the majority of the population viewed them as merely pawns of foreign powers after the 1961 and 1963 elections. Arab landowners were not only part of the power bloc of this newly independent state of Zanzibar but also part of the power bloc of the outgoing British Protectorate. They never established a nationalist ideology supported by institutionalized nationalist development; their hold onto power was always suspect, dependent on the power of the British Empire during the Protectorate period.

The post-independence government failed to satisfy an intellectual and moral leadership that transcended the social divisions of race and class. Rather, they continued a political education for and of their own classes and purposely excluded the majority Africans from the new government and within civil society institutions, such as the police force. In a counter-hegemonic turn of events, the "huge masses...passed suddenly from a state of political passivity to a certain activity, and put forward demands which taken together, albeit not organically formulated, add up to a revolution."[194] Arab and Shirazi landowners failed to fulfill obligations to the newly independent postcolonial state and institute nationalist economic and political reforms that for so long subjugated and marginalized the majority of the population.

Through awareness, class action, material interests, and the charismatic leadership of Okello, mainland African laborers were able to successfully rise up in defense of their class and overthrow the final vestiges of the colonial government. For too long the ruling class had depended entirely upon their relationship to the British in order to maintain power; once the British withdrew, the ruling classes found themselves without a strong partner capable of securing their precarious position in the postcolonial state. As a result, the urban semi-proletariat workers and mainland Africans were able to overthrow the postcolonial government of small and large landowners in one fell swoop.

Bibliography

Adamson, Walter L. *Hegemony and Revolution.* Berkeley: University of California Press, 1980.

Askew, Kelly M. "Female Circles and Male Lines: Gender Dynamics along the Swahili Coast." *Africa Today* 46, no. 3/4 (1999): 67-102.

Ayany, Samuel G. *A History of Zanzibar: A Study in Constitutional Development.* Nairobi: East African Literature Bureau, 1970.

Bennett, Norman R. *A History of the Arab State of Zanzibar.* London: Metheun& Co., 1978.

Bhacker, M. Reda. "Family Strife and Foreign Intervention: Causes in the Separation of Zanzibar from Oman: A Reappraisal." *Bulletin of the School of Oriental and African Studies* (University of London) 54, no. 2 (1991): 269-280.

Bryceson, Deborah Fahy. "The Proletarianization of Women in Tanzania." *Review of African Political Economy* 17 (1980): 4-27.

Burgess, Thomas. "Remembering Youth: Generation in Revolutionary Zanzibar." *Africa Today* 46, no. 2 (1999): 30-44.

Caplan, Pat. "Perceptions of Gender Stratification ." *Africa: Journal of International African Institute* 59, no. 2 (1989): 196-208.

Clayton, Anthony. "The General Strike of Zanzibar." *The Journal of African History* 17, no. 3 (1976): 417-434.

—. *The Zanzibar Revolution and Its Aftermath.* Hamden, CT: Archon Books, 1981.

Constantin, Francois. "Social Stratification on the Swahili Coast: From Race to Class." *Africa: Journal of the International African Institute* 59, no. 2 (1989): 145-160.

Decker, Corrie. "Reading, Writing, and Respectability: How Schoolgirls Developed Modern Literacies in Colonia Zanzibar ." *International Journal of African* 43, no. 1 (2010).

Depelchin, Jacques. "The Transition from Slavery: 1873-1914." In *Zanzibar Under Colonial Rule,* by Abdul and Ed Ferguson Sheriff, 11-35. Athens, Ohio: Ohio University Press, 1991.

Fair, Laura. "Dressing up: Clothing, Class and Gender in Post-Abolition Zanzibar." *The Journal of African History* 39, no. 1 (1998): 63-94.

—. *Pastimes & Politics: Culture, Community, and Identity in Post-*

Abolition Urban Zanzibar 1890-1945. Athens, Ohio: Ohio University Press, 2001.

—. ""It's Just No Fun Anymore": Women's Experiences of Taarab Before and After the 1964 Zanzibar Revolution." *International Journal of African Historical Studies* 35, no. 1 (2002): 61-81.

Feierman, Steven. *Peasant Intellectuals*. Madison: University of Wisconsin, 1990.

Ferguson, Ed. "Value Theory and Colonial Capitalism: The Case of Zanzibar 1897-1945." *African Economic History* 18 (1989): 25-56.

—. "The Formation of the Colonial Economy 1915-1945." In *Zanzibar Under Colonial Rule*, by Abdul and Ed Ferguson Sheriff. Athens, Ohio: Ohio University Press, 1991.

Fontana, Benedetto. "State and Society: The Concept of Hegemony in Gramsci." In *Hegemony and Power*, edited by Mark Haugaard and Howard H Lentner, 23-45. Lanham, MD: Lexington, 2006.

Geiger, Susan. "Women in Nationalist Struggle: TANU Activists in Dar es Salaam." *The International Journal of African Historical Studies* 20, no. 1 (1987): 1-26.

Glassman, Jonathon. "Sorting out the Tribes: The Creation of Racial Identities in Colonial

Zanzibar's Newspaper Wars." *The Journal of African History* 41, no. 3 (2000): 395-428.

Gower, Rebecca, Steven Salm, and Toyin Falola. "Swahili Women Since the Nineteenth Century: Theoretical and Empirical Considerations on Gender and Identity Construction." *Africa Today* 43, no. 3 (Jul-Sept. 1996): 251-268.

Gramsci, Antonio. *Selections from the Prison Notebooks*. Edited by Quintin Hoare and Geoffrey Nowell Smith. New York: International, 1971.

Grandmaison, Colette Le Cour. "Rich Cousins, Poor Cousins: Hidden Stratification among the Omani Arabs in Eastern Africa." *Africa: Journal of the International Africa Institute* 59, no. 2 (1989): 176-184.

Hadivayanis, George and Ed Ferguson. "The Development of the Colonial Working Class." In *Zanzibar Under Colonial Rule*, by Abdul and Ed Ferguson Sheriff, 188-219. Athens, Ohio: Ohio University Press, 1991.

Haugaard, Mark. "Power and Hegemony in Social Theory." In *Hegemony and Power*, edited by Mark Haugaard and Howard H Lentner, 45-64. Lanham, MD: Lexington, 2006.

Haugaard, Mark, and Howard H Lentner,. *Hegemony and Power*. Lanham, MD: Lexington, 2006.

Horton, Mark, and John Middleton. *The Swahili: The Social Landscape of a Mercantile Society*. Oxford: Blackwell, 2000.

Hunt, Alan. *Governing Morals*. Cambridge: Cambridge University Press, 1999.

Ingrams, W.H. *Zanzibar: Its History and Its Peoples*. London: Frank Cass & Co., 1967.

Joseph, Jonathan. *Hegemony: A Realist Analysis*. New York: Routledge, 2002.

Kurki, Milja. *Causation in International Relations*. Cambridge: Cambridge University Press, 2008.

Lofchie, Michael. "Party Conflict in Zanzibar." *The Journal of Modern African Studies* 1, no. 2 (1963): 185-207.

—. *Zanzibar: Background to Revolution*. Princeton: Princeton University Press, 1965.

McCurdy, Sheryl. "Fashioning Sexuality: Desire, Manyema Ethnicity, and the Creation of the 'Kanga' 'ca" 1880-1900." *The International Journal of African Historical Studies* 39, no. 3 (2006): 441-469.

Middleton, John. *Land Tenure in Zanzibar*. London: Her Majesty's Stationery Office, 1961.

Middleton, John, and Jane Campbell. *Zanzibar: Its Society and Politics*. London: Oxford University Press, 1965.

Mlahagwa, J.R and A.J. Temu. "The Decline of the Landlords 1873-1963." In *Zanzibar Under Colonial Rule*, by Abdul and Ed Ferguson Sheriff, 141-162. Athens, Ohio: Ohio University Press, 1991.

Myers, Garth Andrew. "A Stupendous Hammer: Colonial and Post-Colonial Reconstruction of Zanzibar's Other Side." *Urban Studies* 32, no. 8 (1995): 1345-1359.

—. "Sticks and Stone: Colonialism and Zanzibari Housing." *Africa: Journal of the International African Institute* 67, no. 2 (1997): 252-272.

—. "Intellectual of Empire: Eric Dutton and Hegemony in British Africa." *Annals of the Association of American Geographers* 88, no. 1 (1998): 1-27.

Okello, John. *Revolution in Zanzibar*. Nairobi: East African Publishing House, 1967.

Prins, A.H.J. *The Swahili-Speaking Peoples of Zanzibar and the East African Coast*. Bedford: Sidney Press, 1967.

Said, Edward W. *Culture and Imperialism.* New York: Vintage, 1994.

Sanger, Clyde. "Introduction." In *Revolution in Zanzibar,* by John Okello. Nairobi: East African Publishing House, 1967.

Sheriff, Abdul. *Slaves, Spices & Ivory in Zanzibar.* Athens, Ohio: Ohio University Press, 1987.

—. "The Peasantry Under Imperialism." In *Zanzibar Under Colonial Rule,* by Abdul and Ed Ferguson Sheriff. Athens, Ohio: Ohio University Press, 1991.

—. "Race and Class in the Politics in Zanzibar." *Africa Spectrum* 36, no. 3 (2001): 301-318.

Sheriff, Abdul, and Ed Ferguson. *Zanzibar Under Colonial Rule.* Athens, Ohio: Ohio University Press, 1991.

Singer, Shambie. "An Investigation of Land Tenure in Zanzibar." *Anthropos* 91, no. 4/6 (1996): 457-471.

The Economist. "Arabs and Africans." May 17, 1958: 607.

The Economist. "The Headmaster and the Cloves." July 20, 1963: 253.

The Economist. "Zanzibar's Freak Election." January 21, 1961: 241.

Woollacott, Angela. *Gender and Empire.* New York: Palgrave, 2006.

Zanzibar Government. *Blue Book 1945.* Zanzibar: Zanzibar Government Printer, 1945.

Zanzibar Government. *Blue Book 1946.* Zanzibar: Zanzibar Government Printer, 1946.

Zanzibar Government. *Blue Book 1947.* Zanzibar: Zanzibar Government Printer, 1947.

Zanzibar Government. *The Official Gazette of the Zanzibar Government.* Zanizbar : Zanzibar Government, 1953.

Zanzibar Government . *The Official Gazette of the Zanzibar Government .* Zanzibar: Zanzibar Government , 1956.

Zanzibar Government. *Report of the Committee on the Extension of the Franchise to Women.* Zanzibar: Zanzibar Government Press, 1959.

[1] Abdul Sheriff, *Slaves, Spices & Ivory in Zanzibar* (Athens, Ohio: Ohio University Press, 1987), 217.

[2] Samuel G. Ayany, *A History of Zanzibar: A Study in Constitutional Development* (Nairobi: East African Literature Bureau, 1970), 13.

[3] Ibid., 13.

[4] Following the signing of this treaty, "the Sultan retained sovereignty only over the islands of Zanzibar, Pemba, Mafia, and Lamu plus a 16 kilometer coastal strip, about 1608.89 kilometers long, stretching from the Tana River in the north to the Ruvuma in the south. Britain and Germany divided between themselves the hinterland beyond the sixteen kilometer limit by a line drawn from the Umba river westward to Lake Victoria and thus fixed the present boundary between Kenya and Tanganyika." Ibid., 14.

[5] Ibid., 14.

[6] Garth Andrew Myers, "Intellectual of Empire: Eric Dutton and Hegemony in British Africa," *Annals of the Association of American Geographers* 88, no. 1 (1998), 1-27.

[7] Abdul Sheriff, "The Peasantry Under Imperialism," in *Zanzibar Under Colonial Rule* (Athens, Ohio: Ohio University Press, 1991), 109-140.

[8] Antonio Gramsci, *Selections from the Prison Notebooks*, ed. Quintin Hoare and Geoffrey Nowell Smith (New York: International, 1971), 210.

[9] For a full definition of hegemony and its application in this study, see page 33-35 below.

[10] While *shamba* refers to the actual cultivation of a plot of land, *shamba* has also been used to designate the workers engaged in agricultural cultivation; whether this be under slavery, for piece-wage, or for self-sufficiency farming.

[11] See pages 52-53 for the development of waqf

[12] Ferguson in Abdul Sheriff and Ed Ferguson, *Zanzibar Under Colonial Rule* (Athens, Ohio: Ohio University Press, 1991), 36.

[13] Ibid., 36.

[14] Though there is a tendency to associate Gramsci solely with Western capitalist-bourgeois States, this is a limiting perspective that fails to take into account his historical understanding of Italian history prior to and during the Risorgimento, as well as the period leading up to World War I. Recalling Gramsci's numerous writings oriented to the "Southern Question", notably during his period writing for *L'Ordine Nuovo*, it becomes possible to take his Marxist orthodoxy out of solely Western capitalist States (Russia being the greatest example of Marxist orthodoxy applied to a non-Western capitalist State and one that Gramsci understood well) and see his theory as an all consuming answer to the complexities of society. Gramsci of course articulated that all answers to the conditions of society were to be found in Marxism, (Gramsci 462). Zanzibar in particular provides an intriguing study of a pre-capitalist State that was rapidly transitioning from a slave-based cash crop economy to one of a decaying landowning aristocracy who were dependent upon their alliance with the British administration to ensure their power; once that dominance was rescinded during decolonization, the former ruling class had to align themselves with the newly constituted smallholder landowning class. After years of leadership by the British, each class began to emerge; this began within the Arab landowning class, and disseminated itself quickly down to Indian merchants, the African urban proletariat and *shamba* workers. Consciousness came into fruition from within traditional organic communal structures whether they be football or dance associations (generally the former were composed of men and the latter of women), trade unions, or tenants associations. These were formed in opposition to the economic domination of the landowning classes, as well as political-educational

institutions of the Protectorate, which privileged the ruling group at the expense of the lower classes. These communal associations allowed for actors to first loosely align themselves and provided access, however limited, for agency of individuals. Gramsci notes that hegemonic forces form within institutions of civil society that are able to function outside of the control of the State, but are still subject to their influences, notably economic and political. The weakness of civil society institutions, which are not able to fully form outside of bourgeois capitalist systems, do not in themselves provide the opportunity for hegemony, but are merely vehicles through which alliances are able to form between classes. Whether these hegemonic forces are successful in overthrowing the domination of the ruling class depends upon whether or not the ruling class is able to maintain both hegemony and dominance within the State. See also: Steven Feierman, *Peasant Intellectuals* (Madison: University of Wisconsin, 1990).

[15] "Hegemonies always grow out of historical blocs...not all historical blocs are hegemonic... its political alliances with other such groups may or may not develop into a hegemonic relationship." Moreover, though the established ruling class may form political alliances with other classes they "may or may not develop into a hegemonic relationship" as such, but rather one of mutual benefit or need. It is only through the "intermeshing or structure and superstructure inherent in the definition of the historic bloc itself" that such an alliance can come to constitute a historic bloc. From: Walter L. Adamson *Hegemony and Revolution* (Berkeley: University of California Press, 1980), 177-78.

[16] Gramsci, *Selections from the Prison Notebooks*, 250.

[17] Sheriff, *Zanzibar Under Colonial Rule*, 21-23.

[18] Norman R. Bennett, *A History of the Arab State of Zanzibar* (London: Metheun& Co., 1978), 235.

[19] Michael F. Lofchie, *Zanzibar: Background to Revolution* (Princeton: Princeton University Press, 1965), 9.

[20] Ed Ferguson, "The Formation of the Colonial Economy 1915-1945," in *Zanzibar Under Colonial Rule* (Athens, Ohio: Ohio University Press, 1991).

[21] Gramsci (1971), 53.

[22] "The political moment is connected to the economic moment, though by a long and complex chain of mediations..." Adamson, *Hegemony and Revolution*, 206.

[23] Sheriff, *Zanzibar Under Colonial Rule*, 120.

[24] Ibid., 334.

[25] Adamson, *Hegemony and Revolution*, 178.

[26] Sheriff, *Slaves, Spices & Ivory in Zanzibar*.

[27] "A tradesman does not join a political party in order to do business, nor an industrialist in order to produce more at lower cost, nor a peasant to learn new methods of cultivation, even if some aspects of these demands of the tradesman, the industrialist or the peasant can find satisfaction in the party," Gramsci, *Selections from the Prison Notebooks*, 16.

[28] See Sheriff, *Zanzibar Under Colonial Rule*, 36-40.

[29] See page 76 and footnote 139.

[30] See meeting of the Legislative Council, November 18, 1953: Zanzibar Government, *The Official Gazette of the Zanzibar Government*, (Zanizbar : Zanzibar Government, 1953).

[31] Francois Constantin, "Social Stratification on the Swahili Coast: From Race to Class," *Africa: Journal of the International African Institute* 59, no. 2 (1989), 146.

[32] Gramsci, *Selections from the Prison Notebooks*, 63.

[33] Ibid., 133.

[34] Ibid., 133.

[35] Ibid., 276.

[36] Ayany, *A History of Zanzibar: A Study in Constitutional Development*, 13.

[37] See John Middleton, *Land Tenure in Zanzibar* (London: Her Majesty's Stationery Office, 1961). Middleton does not attempt to theorize what occurred prior to Sultan Sayyid Said as the information is scant. However, by looking at the situation in the late 1950s to early 1960, he is able to conclude differences and similarities between Zanzibar and Pemba outside of Zanzibar Town, which is where most scholars have concentrated their research. While Zanzibar and Pemba are similar in many respects, Middleton highlights important differences. He notes that the population is much more ethnically mixed than in Zanzibar with Arabs and Africans (Shirazi) intermarrying. Unlike in Zanzibar, the Arabs of Pemba are often smallholders and farmers or fishermen; large-scale plantations, though they do exist in Pemba and are mainly owned by Arabs, are relatively few compared with majority smallholdings of Arabs and Africans (Shirazi). Pemba also experienced significant immigration from mainland Africa and has a more mixed population of mainland Africans, Shirazi Africans, and Arabs. The overall composition of climate on Pemba is slightly different than Zanzibar and has contributed, so Middleton believes, to a more mobile population. There is no comparison of a large city like Zanzibar Town on Pemba, though there are small cities, the majority of the population lives in small settlements scattered across the island and are largely removed from the administrative regulations of Zanzibar Town.

[38] Also worth noting at this time was the catastrophic hurricane in April 1872 which damaged many of the clove trees on Zanzibar island while leaving Pemba island relatively unscathed. According to Middleton, Pemba became far more important than Zanzibar island in clove production since clove trees take at least a decade to fully grow and do not reach their strongest yields until about thirty years of age; at the same time, due to intermarriage of Arabs and Africans, the profusion of small holdings continued to rise as the devastation on Zanzibar provided a boom to the landowners and clove growers in Pemba, allowing them to increase their holdings.

[39] Ayany, *A History of Zanzibar: A Study in Constitutional Development*, 20.

[40] From roughly April to October there occurs the Southwest Monsoon, which is usually when goods and slaves would arrive; exports of cloves and slaves would occur during the Northeast Monsoon from November to March.

[41] Jacques Depelchin, "The Transition from Slavery: 1873-1914," in *Zanzibar Under Colonial Rule*, 11-35 (Athens, Ohio: Ohio University Press, 1991).

[42] Norman R. Bennett, *A History of the Arab State of Zanzibar* (London: Metheun& Co., 1978), 166.

[43] Ibid.,167-68.

[44] Ibid., 166.

[45] Depelchin, "The Transition from Slavery: 1873-1914," 21.

[46] Ibid., 26.

[47] Bennett, *A History of the Arab State of Zanzibar*, 182.

[48] Depelchin, "The Transition from Slavery: 1873-1914," 27.

[49] Ibid., 29.

[50] Abdul Sheriff, "Race and Class in the Politics in Zanzibar," *Africa Spectrum* 36, no. 3 (2001), 303.

[51] Laura Fair, *Pastimes & Politics: Culture, Community, and Identity in Post-Abolition Urban Zanzibar 1890-1945* (Athens, Ohio: Ohio University Press, 2001), 38-41

[52] J.R and A.J. Temu Mlahagwa, "The Decline of the Landlords 1873-1963," in *Zanzibar Under Colonial Rule*, 141-162 (Athens, Ohio: Ohio University Press, 1991).

[53] As will be made clear, there existed non-hegemonic rule in colonial Zanzibar that appears, at times, to be hegemonic, but was not fully invested as such until the "time of politics" following the aftermath of World War II. Rather, the Protectorate was able to rule as such through domination, not in the manner of an authoritarian dictatorship, but rather through domination that is specific to colonial regimes. This requires that the preceding structures of power are not removed, which would culminate into chaos and resistance, but rather subjugating a weakened or non-existent opposition who remain unable to channel agency or establish hegemony through civil society. The weakness of civil society, through which former slaves would have been able to form alliances with other classes in order to constitute a historic bloc, further points to the lack of hegemony.

[54] Adamson, *Hegemony and Revolution*, 169-178.

[55] Gramsci, *Selections from the Prison Notebooks*, 57.

[56] Ibid., 57.

[57] Ibid., 59.

[58] Adamson, *Hegemony and Revolution*, 169-178.

[59] The Protectorate employed coercive measures, in policy, until 1916, but continued to enact practices, such as labor contracts favoring the landowners, until the 1950s. These measures in the period following abolition were employed to force the large labor force of *shamba* farmers to work, for a wage, during harvesting seasons. See, Sheriff, "The Peasantry Under Imperialism," 120-121.

[60] Adamson, *Hegemony and Revolution*, 178.

[61] "There is a danger is equating ethnic origins with class positions in Zanzibar society. What is determinant in relations of production is class position, the class position and not the ethnic origin. The danger resides in substituting ethnic solidarity for class solidarity," Sheriff, *Zanzibar Under Colonial Rule*, 12-13.

[62] Prior to the abolishment of slavery, the economic conditions of labor exploitation did not allow for the establishment of independent associations for communal representation. Only by creating a system in which surplus value could become accumulated, however limited that surplus value may be, could these associations come to function with a limited degree of independence. By ensuring that they were not dependent upon the economic privileges of the colonial state, these associations conferred themselves to fostering power within communities through their practices.

[63] Sheriff, "The Peasantry Under Imperialism," 123.

[64] Bennett, *A History of the Arab State of Zanzibar*, 202

[65] Ed Ferguson, "Value Theory and Colonial Capitalism: The Case of Zanzibar 1897-1945," *African Economic History* 18 (1989), 25-56.

[66] "Whereas the expanded reproduction of capital required an ever expanding labour population, the reproduction of slave labour was becoming financially prohibitive. Furthermore, the large slave population…required a repressive apparatus with the means to suppress any attempt at revolt," Sheriff, *Zanzibar Under Colonial Rule*, 21-22.

[67] Gramsci, *Selections from the Prison Notebooks*, 12.

[68] Sheriff, *Zanzibar Under Colonial Rule*, 40.

[69] Ibid., 28.

[70] "Identity of terms does not mean identity of concepts," Gramsci, *Selections from the Prison Notebooks*, 456.

[71] Ibid., 53.

[72] Ibid., 80,f49

[73] Ibid., 160.

[74] Ibid., 161.

[75] Ibid., 299.

[76] See Ferguson, "The Formation of the Colonial Economy 1915-1945," 40-60.

[77] Sheriff, *Zanzibar Under Colonial Rule*, 41.

[78] Ed Ferguson, "Value Theory and Colonial Capitalism: The Case of Zanzibar 1897-1945," *African Economic History* 18 (1989), 27.

[79] "The state obtained its revenue primarily from taxes, and to a lesser extent from rents, fees, licenses and interest. The tax on exports and imports, or customs revenue, was the most important source...in 1899 at 5 percent of value, and was raised to 7.5 percent in 1907, 10 percent in 1921, and 15 percent in 1927." Ibid., 47.

[80] Jonathan Joseph, *Hegemony: A Realist Analysis* (New York: Routledge, 2002), 35.

[81] Sheriff, *Slaves, Spices & Ivory in Zanzibar*, 67.

[82] Joseph, *Hegemony: A Realist Analysis*, 67.

[83] According to Bennett: "The policy was clearly expressed in the mid 1920s when reforms were made concerning the subordinate levels of local administration. The government claimed that it planned 'as far as possible to appoint Arabs' to vacancies in lower staff positions," *A History of the Arab State of Zanzibar*, 235.

[84] Sheriff, *Zanzibar Under Colonial Rule*, 179.

[85] Fair, *Pastimes & Politics: Culture, Community, and Identity in Post-Abolition Urban Zanzibar 1890-1945*, 123.

[86] Ibid., 124.

[87] Ibid., 123.

[88] Ibid., 134-5.

[89] Bennett, *A History of the Arab State of Zanzibar*, 235.

[90] See: Mark Horton and John Middleton, *The Swahili: The Social Landscape of a Mercantile Society* (Oxford: Blackwell, 2000). Francois Constantin, "Social Stratification on the Swahili Coast: From Race to Class," *Africa: Journal of the International African Institute* 59, no. 2 (1989), 145-160. Kelly M. Askew, "Female Circles and Male Lines: Gender Dynamics along the Swahili Coast," *Africa Today* 46, no. 3/4 (1999), 67-102.

[91] Francois Constantin, "Social Stratification on the Swahili Coast: From Race to Class," *Africa: Journal of the International African Institute* 59, no. 2 (1989), 148.

[92] Ethnicity "could be adopted as necessary to meet the particular social, economic, and political goals of the human actors as they negotiated their way through the complexities of real life," Fair, *Pastimes & Politics: Culture, Community, and Identity in Post-Abolition Urban Zanzibar 1890-1945*, 29.

[93] Angela Woollacott, *Gender and Empire* (New York: Palgrave, 2006).

[94] Myers, "Intellectual of Empire: Eric Dutton and Hegemony in British Africa," 6.

[95] Fair, *Pastimes & Politics: Culture, Community, and Identity in Post-Abolition Urban Zanzibar 1890-1945*, 38-9.

[96] Ibid., 39.

[97] Jonathon Glassman, "Sorting out the Tribes: The Creation of Racial Identities in Colonial Zanzibar's Newspaper Wars," *The Journal of African History* 41, no. 3 (2000), 402-3.

[98] Fair, *Pastimes & Politics: Culture, Community, and Identity in Post-Abolition Urban Zanzibar 1890-1945*, 28.

[99] Gramsci, *Selections from the Prison Notebooks*, 334.

[100] Ibid., 335.

[101] Samuel G. Ayany, *A History of Zanzibar: A Study in Constitutional Development* (Nairobi: East African Literature Bureau, 1970).

[102] Fair, *Pastimes & Politics: Culture, Community, and Identity in Post-Abolition Urban Zanzibar 1890-1945*, 45; Middleton, *Land Tenure in Zanzibar*, 6.

[103] Sheriff, "The Peasantry Under Imperialism," 86.

[104] Fair, *Pastimes & Politics: Culture, Community, and Identity in Post-Abolition Urban Zanzibar 1890-1945*, 134-5.

[105] See page 74.

[106] Bennett, *A History of the Arab State of Zanzibar*, 214.

[107] "The only indigenous community singled out for even a limited role in the political life of the islands was the Arabs, the result of the continuing British perception of Zanzibar as being primarily an Arab state." Ibid., 235.

[108] Gramsci, *Selections from the Prison Notebooks*, 151.

[109] Ibid., 151.

[110] Ibid., 148.

[111] Bennett, *A History of the Arab State of Zanzibar*, 203.

[112] Gramsci, *Selections from the Prison Notebooks*, 227.

[113] See discussion of Gramsci's nonhegemonic systems and the "pseudohegemonic situation" in Adamson, *Hegemony and Revolution*, 174-76.

[114] Lofchie, *Zanzibar: Background to Revolution*, 187.

[115] Ibid., 247.

[116] Ibid., 247.

[117] George and Ed Ferguson Hadivayanis, "The Development of the Colonial Working Class," in *Zanzibar Under Colonial Rule*, (Athens, Ohio: Ohio University Press, 1991), 188-219.

[118] Fair, *Pastimes & Politics: Culture, Community, and Identity in Post-Abolition Urban Zanzibar 1890-1945*, 21.

[119] Ibid., 38-9.

[120] Ferguson "The Formation of the Colonial Economy 1915-1945," 69.

[121] Ibid., 54.

[122] John Middleton and Jane Campbell, *Zanzibar: Its Society and Politics* (London: Oxford University Press, 1965), 35-39.

[123] Ibid., 39.

[124] Ibid., 35.

[125] Fair, *Pastimes & Politics: Culture, Community, and Identity in Post-Abolition Urban Zanzibar 1890-1945*, 45.

[126] Lofchie, *Zanzibar: Background to Revolution*, 82.

[127] Gramsci, *Selections from the Prison Notebooks*, 334.

[128] "Boycotts are a form of war of movement, strikes are war of movement..." Ibid., 229.

[129] For further reading on Ng'ambo and Stone Town see: Laura Fair, *Pastimes & Politics: Culture, Community, and Identity in Post-Abolition Urban Zanzibar 1890-1945* (Athens, Ohio: Ohio University Press, 2001); Garth Andrew Myers, "Sticks and Stone: Colonialism and Zanzibari Housing," *Africa: Journal of the International African Institute* 67, no. 2 (1997), 252-272; Garth Andrew Myers, "A Stupendous Hammer: Colonial and Post-Colonial Reconstruction of Zanzibar's Other Side," *Urban Studies* 32, no. 8 (1995), 1345-1359; Garth Andrew Myers, "Intellectual of Empire: Eric Dutton and Hegemony in British Africa," *Annals of the Association of American Geographers* 88, no. 1 (1998), 1-27.

[130] Fair, *Pastimes & Politics: Culture, Community, and Identity in Post-Abolition Urban Zanzibar 1890-1945*, 149.

[131] Myers, "Sticks and Stone: Colonialism and Zanzibari Housing," 260-1.

[132] Bennett, *A History of the Arab State of Zanzibar*, 203.

[133] Ibid., 209.

[134] Ibid., 212.

[135] Ibid., 235.

[136] "The problem confronting the British administrators was that any effective remedy for Arab indebtedness might offend the economic interests of the Asian community. Official determination to restore the Arab oligarchy to solvency would thus have profound political consequences," Lofchie, *Zanzibar: Background to Revolution*, 114.

[137] Ibid., 119.

[138] Adamson, *Hegemony and Revolution*, 178-9.

[139] The war of movement, or maneuver, as well as the war of position, is articulated by Gramsci, *Selections from the Prison Notebooks*, 108-110, 229-235, 237-239.

[140] Lofchie, *Zanzibar: Background to Revolution*, 126.

[141] Fair, *Pastimes & Politics: Culture, Community, and Identity in Post-Abolition Urban Zanzibar 1890-1945*, 161.

[142] Gramsci, *Selections from the Prison Notebooks*, 232.

[143] Fair, *Pastimes & Politics: Culture, Community, and Identity in Post-Abolition Urban Zanzibar 1890-1945*, 48.

[144] Lofchie, *Zanzibar: Background to Revolution*, 130.

[145] It is well worth noting that in discussion the various racial associations that must be described by their connotation with a particular racial group (Arab, Indian/Asian, and African) regardless of the fact of whether they actually represented the interests of their community. As has been noted throughout this review, the class-based divisions of the population are not clear-cut and are deeply obscured by the colonial practice of divide and rule. For example, the Arab Association, though

it claimed to represent Arabs as a collective group, only articulated the interests of the landowning elite within the Arab community. Less than 2 per cent of Arabs were large-scale landowners, the rest of the community being anywhere from subsistence peasant farmers to civil servants to petite-bourgeoisie landlords. The complex class relationships that existed within these racial communities have largely been ignored by many scholars, who have tended to pose divisions based solely on ethnic tensions. For further readings, see: Colette Le Cour Grandmaison, "Rich Cousins, Poor Cousins: Hidden Stratification among the Omani Arabs in Eastern Africa," *Africa: Journal of the International Africa Institute* 59, no. 2 (1989), 176-184; Francois Constantin, "Social Stratification on the Swahili Coast: From Race to Class," *Africa: Journal of the International African Institute* 59, no. 2 (1989), 145-160; Kelly M. Askew, "Female Circles and Male Lines: Gender Dynamics along the Swahili Coast," *Africa Today* 46, no. 3/4 (1999), 67-102; A.H.J Prins, *The Swahili-Speaking Peoples of Zanzibar and the East African Coast* (Bedford: Sidney Press, 1967).

[146] Fair, *Pastimes & Politics: Culture, Community, and Identity in Post-Abolition Urban Zanzibar 1890-1945*, 48-55.

[147] Ibid., 8-9.

[148] Ibid., 51.

[149] Laura Fair, "It's Just No Fun Anymore": Women's Experiences of Taarab Before and After the 1964 Zanzibar Revolution," *International Journal of African Historical Studies* 35, no. 1 (2002), 61-81.

[150] Fair, *Pastimes & Politics: Culture, Community, and Identity in Post-Abolition Urban Zanzibar 1890-1945*, 24.

[151] Fair, "It's Just No Fun Anymore": Women's Experiences of Taarab Before and After the 1964 Zanzibar Revolution," 62.

[152] Gramsci, *Selections from the Prison Notebooks*, 210.

[153] Sheriff, *Zanzibar Under Colonial Rule*, 86.

[154] Lofchie, *Zanzibar: Background to Revolution*, 131-2.

[155] Zanzibar Government, *The Official Gazette of the Zanzibar Government*, (Zanzibar: Zanzibar Government,1956), 7.

[156] For further reading on the 1948 General Strike see: Anthony Clayton, "The General Strike of Zanzibar," *The Journal of African History* 17, no. 3 (1976), 417-434; Anthony Clayton, *The Zanzibar Revolution and Its Aftermath* (Hamden, CT: Archon Books, 1981).

[157] Clayton, "The General Strike of Zanzibar," 6.

[158] Ibid., 32.

[159] Ibid., 34.

[160] Ibid., 37.

[161] Ibid., 39.

[162] Mark Horton and John Middleton, *The Swahili: The Social Landscape of a Mercantile Society* (Oxford: Blackwell, 2000).

[163] Lofchie, *Zanzibar: Background to Revolution*, 249.

[164] Ibid., 165.

[165] Michael Lofchie, "Party Conflict in Zanzibar," *The Journal of Modern African Studies* 1, no. 2 (1963), 190.

[166] "A nationalist party in the colonial setting has the goal of mobilizing all classes as a nation

against foreign rule…nationalist parties were created by propertied individuals, large and small, with a bourgeois class position." Sheriff, *Zanzibar Under Colonial Rule*, 205.

[167] Middleton and Campbell, *Zanzibar: Its Society and Politics*, 47.

[168] Lofchie, "Party Conflict in Zanzibar," 190.

[169] Zanzibar Government, *The Official Gazette of the Zanzibar Government*, (Zanzibar: Zanzibar Government, 1956), 7.

[170] The ZNP was born out of the remains of the National Party of the Subjects of the Sultan of Zanzibar (NPSS). The NPSS was formed in mid-1955, during the Arab boycott of the Legislative Council, by "a small group of peasants in the village of Kiembe Samaki…their party possessed a multi-racial ideology with an appeal for an end to communal representation in the Legislative Council and a demand for independence." Lofchie, *Zanzibar: Background to Revolution*,147-8. The peasant origins of the ZNP was an important factor for the Arab leadership in attempting to appeal to the broadest possible segments of the population in order to transcend ethnic and class divisions.

[171] Middleton and Campbell, *Zanzibar: Its Society and Politics*, 47.

[172] Lofchie,"Party Conflict in Zanzibar," 197.

[173] *The Economist*, "Arabs and Africans," May 17,1958, 607.

[174] There are hinted references that the ZNP may have held close ties to the emerging pan-Arabism of Nasserism. While it is not for the study of this paper to devote attention to this, it is interesting to note that the platform of the ZNP was a sharp and immediate break from their sixty-seven year alliance with the colonial administration. Whether the ZNP was directly influenced by the spread of Nasser's influence or, as is more likely, the ZNP had decided that the best route to retaining their power domination was through establishing a power bloc with the dissenting Shirazi Association landowners. See: John Okello, *Revolution in Zanzibar* (Nairobi: East African Publishing House, 1967); Norman R. Bennett, *A History of the Arab State of Zanzibar* (London: Metheun& Co.,1978).

[175] There are conflicting details as to whether the split occurred in December 1959, as cited in Middleton and Campbell, *Zanzibar: Its Society and Politics*, 54, or in March 1960 as cited by Okello, *Revolution in Zanzibar*, 79. Since Okello was writing his memoir from prison with the aid of his memory, I will favor the former source as the more credible one. Also, the term ASP seems to be substituted by many authors when recounting the 1957 election even though the ASP did not actually exist until the split of the ASU into two distinct parties.

[176] Lofchie, *Zanzibar: Background to Revolution*, 243.

[177] Ibid., 187.

[178] Jonathon Glassman, "Sorting out the Tribes: The Creation of Racial Identities in Colonial Zanzibar's Newspaper Wars," *The Journal of African History* 41, no. 3 (2000), 395-428.

[179] Lofchie, *Zanzibar: Background to Revolution*, 224.

[180] Ibid., 224.

[181] See table 10.

[182] Middleton and Campbell, *Zanzibar: Its Society and Politics*, 56.

[183] Between the elections of July 1957 and those of June 1961, the electorate had increased from around 32,000 voters to 89,264. This was the result of the extension of franchise to women in 1959, as well as removal of restrictions on voting based on landownership and education. By the time final elections were held in July 1963, the number of voters stood at 160,000. Further reading: Zanzibar Government, *Report of the Committee on the Extension of the Franchise to Women*, (Zanzibar: Zanzibar Government Press, 1959).

[184] Bennett, *A History of the Arab State of Zanzibar*, 261.

[185] Lofchie, "Party Conflict in Zanzibar," 186.

[186] Ibid., 271.

[187] Clyde Sanger, "Introduction," in *Revolution in Zanzibar* (Nairobi: East Africa Publishing House, 1967), 15-19.

[188] Mainland Africans were commonly employed in the police force and made up the majority of the policemen on the islands.

[189] Okello, *Revolution in Zanzibar*, 85. To note, there has been various dissenting views of Okello's account of the revolution, most notably the immediate aftermath and the circumstances surrounding his exclusion from power by the Revolutionary government. Rumors circulating at the time also claimed that Okello was a communist revolutionary who had been trained in Cuba; these are most likely false. However, the events of the revolution, as documented by the ASP, largely dismiss Okello as a leader, with some accounts branding him as a traitor. To what extent Okello's account is true can only be measured by the faith in any first-hand account of a violent and momentous event. Nevertheless, Okello's book is genuinely fascinating as a personal account of a revolutionary.

[190] Ibid., 98.

[191] Gramsci, *Selections from the Prison Notebooks*, 196-200.

[192] Ibid., 197.

[193] Accounts of rape, torture, and mass murder of much of the Arab population have been extensively documented and debated. In his book, Okello justifies his behavior as retribution for past injustices against Africans by Arabs, as well as politically necessary for the removal of the ruling class. I do not in anyway agree with or condone Okello's actions; nor do I believe that by applying Gramscian terms to Okello I am justifying him. However, his role as an enigmatic, skillful leader in the facilitating the Revolution is useful study.

[194] Gramsci, *Selections from the Prison Notebooks*, 210.

CPSIA information can be obtained
at www.ICGtesting.com
Printed in the USA
LVHW032220111121
703078LV00008B/1389